HARTLY HOUSE
CALCUTTA

A NOVEL OF THE DAYS OF
WARREN HASTINGS

Anonymous

Introduction and Notes by Monica Clough

PLUTO PRESS

London   •   Winchester, Mass

This edition first published 1989 by Pluto Press
345 Archway Road, London N6 5AA
and 8 Winchester Place, Winchester MA 01890, USA

First published in 1789

British Library Cataloguing in Publication Data

Hartly House, Calcutta.—(Writers abroad).
I. Series
823'.6   PR4759.H63/
ISBN 1-85305-070-9

Library of Congress Cataloging-in-Publication Data

Hartly House, Calcutta / anonymous ; introduced by Monica Clough.
    p.   cm.
  ISBN 1-85305-070-9
  1. India–History–18th century–Fiction. 2. Hastings, Warren,
1732-1818–Fiction. I. Clough, Monica.
PR3991.A1H3 1988
823'.6–dc19   87-20746
                                                        CIP

CONTENTS

INTRODUCTION

MONICA CLOUGH

––––––––––

The actual copy of *Hartly House, Calcutta,* reproduced for this reissue, was picked up about 40 years ago in one of many forays round the dusty stacks of the second-hand booksellers of Dhurramtollah Street, Calcutta. So was the copy of *The European in India* from which the cover illustration is taken. Both books help an understanding of the curious life led by our British predecessors in Bengal in the eighteenth century. *Hartly House* is a novel which repays careful reading on several levels. No one could make great claims for it as literature. It is not even particularly accurate in some of the details of the Calcutta it sets out to describe. Nevertheless the broad assumptions made by the author about the society, both British and Bengali, against which she sets her story are important and very different from the stereotype of the Imperial Raj with which we have become familiar. *Hartly House, Calcutta* was first published anonymously in London in 1789, in three volumes by Dodwell, and an apparently pirated edition followed in

Dublin in the same year. Two years later a German translation appeared in Leipzig, and the edition from which the present volume has been produced came out in Calcutta in 1908.

The story is told through a series of descriptive letters to a female friend written by the heroine, Sophia Goldborne, who accompanies her father to Calcutta, landing in September 1784 and leaving again in March 1786. As a literary device letters had become old fashioned even in the 1780s. The author alternates paragraphs of girlish stuff (such as her resolve never to quit her father's side: we know what is likely to happen to the maker, on the first page or two of a three-decker novel, of such a resolution) with serious attempts to describe the customs of Calcutta and the Hartly household in which she is staying. These alternations between the arch and the informative make for uneven progress through the book, but gradually the personality of Sophia becomes endearingly familiar. The effect is much as if an earlier Emma Woodhouse ('handsome, clever and rich') had gone East and written to tell her dim friend Harriet of her social triumphs and her new experiences. Arabella, recipient of these confidences, never assumes any identity, nor does the author hit off much character in her hosts, Mr and Mrs Hartly, who are 'benevolent'. Nor does she really differentiate between her train of admirers. Her eventual fate, the

Edmund Doyly who wins her father's consent, a fortune and her hand, in that order, is an inarticulate paragon. On meeting him she finds 'his Person is pastoral and his sensibility is Oriental' – Doyly is an avowed second best. By the time Sophia leaves Calcutta, eighteen months after her arrival, she has fallen in love with a young Bengali Bramin, and become deeply attracted by hindu India. She nearly dies of fever, her Bramin does die, and at the end of the book she tells Arabella: 'So altered am I in my views that I have settled with myself to affect the Gentoo [hindu] air, which is an assemblage of all the soft winning graces priests and poets have yet devised a name for, and Doyly shall figure away as my Bramin.' The fact that in the preceding paragraph she has promised to bring home 'large assortments of Eastern manufactures' – Cashmir shawls and Indian jewellery – should not disguise the underlying seriousness of the theme. Hidden under a great deal of conventional posturing, written with high spirits and youthful naïvety, there is a genuine attempt to understand the India under her gaze. Furthermore, the British assumptions from which she starts in India have been so overlaid by our more recent concepts of the Imperial Raj that it is a shock to recognise the cool rationality, the Voltairean rejection of organised Christianity and the readiness to admire, to concede excellence to

Indian customs and hindu beliefs that characterised the British in the last quarter of the eighteenth century, the Age of Reason, in Calcutta. How typically Sophia reflected all of British society there it is impossible to say. The dates of her visit are so clearly given that we can be precise, and can check her accounts of the Governor's leave-takings, and of nabob's visits, of theatre performances and of newspapers and can confirm the identities of most of her public characters, from many later publications. Footnotes at the end of the book contain much of the detail which may be needed to elucidate her narrative.

And how typical was 'my Bramin'? He is never given a name perhaps because Bengali Bramin family names are as recognisable as those of the handful of Highland clans. The platonic love affair is outlined with a delicacy and precision that is largely absent from the rest of the book. Its course makes clear the great divide between the early Company days and the later Raj. Sophia and Mrs Hartly have the Bramin to tea, with an interpreter, and Sophia sets her cap at him: 'An admirer of his character would be to me a proof of my attractions I should be proud of' (p. 89). (Some of her British admirers were less praiseworthy, though the drunken fellow who tries to kiss her hand from a neighbouring boat, and tips himself and the other suitor into the Hoogly does have some panache.) The Bramin is represented as the nephew of her father's *Sekar*, his hindu 'broker, notary or factor ... and though such inter- course is unusual, [the Sekar] has attached himself to his employer by the heartfelt ties of friendship and affection – walks in and out of Hartly House at pleasure and converses by signs with me, with many marks of high approbation'. How unusual is not clear; any factotum who walked into his employer's house and made unmistakable gestures of approbation of his daughter in later times would have been put off the verandah, fast. But the acquaintance with his nephew ripens, fostered by Sophia's genuine interest in hindu tenets, and in one case by her ignorance of them. She believes 'her Bramin' to be vowed to celibacy, together with most of his brethren: 'little inferior to the purity and benignity of angels'. This leads her to discuss the caste structure, and to outline her understanding of 'her Bramin's' teaching, which remarkably anticipates the later teaching of Ram Mohan Roy, founder of the *Bramho Samaj* movement a generation later: a hinduism of *ahimsa*, of non-violence purged of gross idolatry, grounded in a belief in the all-embracing supremacy of Brahma. Neither her father nor her hostess, Mrs Hartly, nor any other minor character find this attachment alarming nor do they make any attempt to thwart its progress. Sophia is a well-read girl and soon understands that a belief in reincarnation is a mainspring of hindu life: 'the doctrine of the metemsy-chosis is to me the religion of humanity', she cries. She is very much the modern woman of the 1780s, and the 'religion of humanity' is her key note. She dismisses the antics of the Presidency Chaplain with caustic wit, and soon after arrival she writes: 'Ashamed of the manners of modern Christianity (amongst the professors of which, acts of devotion are subjects of ridicule, and charity in all its amiable branches, a polite jest), I am become a convert to the Gentoo faith, and have my Bramin to instruct me *per diem*.' It is not surprising that a novel which runs so counter to the later hostility of the British to any Indian way of life should have vanished from the bookshelves and been almost forgotten or suppressed. Her search for a guru would shock many later generations in British India. Sophia, however, arrived in Calcutta when Warren Hastings was winding up his thirteen years as Governor of Bengal and less censorious attitudes prevailed. For a detailed discussion of 'Sophia and the Bramin' the reader is referred to A L Basham's paper.[1]

Taking a broad look at the background to our under-standing of this book, Warren Hastings governed a Presidency where corrupt British merchants had stripped the richest Province of India for personal gain, and its Mogul administration had become a wreck. No apologist can make out a good case for British behaviour in the 1760s. Hastings set out lasting reforms; though he was handicapped by a hostile Council, a greedy cadre of officers, and a distant Board of Directors in London, six months' journey away. His attitude to government by cooperation with Indians is implicit in this book. For an understanding of Sophia's Calcutta, however, it is only necessary to say that in his time Hastings encouraged the earliest work of British Oriental scholars, and he himself spoke and wrote Court Persian, the language of Mogul government, Bengali, Urdu, and a little Arabic. The Orientalists laid the foundation for the Bengali renaissance by their careful rescue, translation and publication of much Sanskrit writing, which was in danger of being lost. Halhed published the first *Code of Hindu Law* with the help of ten pundits, Wilkins translated the *Gita* and Sir William Jones, a judge, founded the Asiatic Society of Bengal in 1784, under Hastings' auspices, and went on to shake Western scholars by convincingly arguing a common origin for all Indo-European languages. The first presses in India were already printing vernacular work, under Hastings' encouragement. The Orientalists whom he fostered 'evoked a golden age in India's cultural past and they shared their discoveries with the native intelligentsia of Bengal. Racial privilege was anathema to them. They were rationalists, grounded in the classics and ... they believed that both races in

India had much to give to each other.'[2] Sophia, the heroine of *Hartly House*, makes no direct mention of these pundits, but she writes in their shadow. And she echoes almost uncannily a few lines of Hastings' on the hindu peoples:

> They are gentle, benevolent, more susceptible of gratitude for kindness shewn them than prompt to vengeance for wrongs sustained, abhorrent of bloodshed ... superstitious, but they do not think ill of us for not behaving as they do ... The least therefore that can be expected of the most liberal and enlightened of all nations that providence has appointed as the guardian of their civil rights, is to protect their persons from wrong and to leave their religious creed to the Being who has so long endured it and who will in his own time reform it.[3]

However, the climate of opinion in Britain was even then altering from a tolerance of alien faiths to an evangelical zeal for conversion. The seeds of intolerance were already in Calcutta, in the shape of young Mr Charles Grant, with an appointment in the Calcutta Board of Trade, and his wife. They suffered the loss of their children from cholera, in a night, and had swung under the blow to the then unfashionable consolations of evangelical piety. Grant went home to

London in 1790 (with a comfortable fortune) and rose to become an MP in the India interest, and eventually President of the Board of Directors of the East India Company. At the same time he was a member of the Clapham sect of Evangelicals, men who included reformers such as Wilberforce and fanatics such as Zaccary Macaulay. They were all bitterly opposed to the orientalising of Hastings, and later of Wellesley, whose Calcutta College designed to educate the young entrants to the Company's service in Indian law and languages they succeeded in transferring to the safe pastures of Haileybury in Essex. Eventually in 1813, on the renewal of the East India Company's Charter, Grant managed to persuade Parliament to agree to a measure to set up Anglican sees in India and to allow formerly forbidden missionary endeavour. Bishop Heber was sent out and his lines 'From Greenland's icy mountains to India's coral strand ... They call us to deliver/Their land from error's chain' became the battle-hymn of 100 years of missionary endeavour, sadly allied to a misunderstanding of and contempt for Indian habits of thought. The evangelicals were rein-forced by a new generation of memsahibs from England, reared in the piety which was the reaction to Regency levity and humanism and by a younger Macaulay's famous Minute dismissing the whole of Indian culture in favour of an English education.

When Kipling wrote *Kim* over 100 years after our author, he gave a telling thumb-nail sketch of Bennet the chaplain, who looked at the Red-hat Lama 'with the triple-ringed uninterest of the creed that lumps nine-tenths of the world under the title of "heathen"'. It is a relief to return to the Calcutta of Sophia in 1786, although one feels she would have approved of our historical scene-setting. She was prone to this too.

Sophia herself is given as an authority on Calcutta by H E Busteed, in his *Echoes From Old Calcutta*.[4] In several instances he quotes verbatim from *Hartly House* but attributes the material to Mrs Fay, a contemporary of Sophia's whose *Letters* were not published until long afterwards. Nor does Busteed remark that *Hartly House* is a novel. As Busteed is a much used source of information about the eighteenth century in Calcutta it is important to point out how much he has relied on a work of fiction for his chapter on home and social life.

It remains to be considered who wrote *Hartly House, Calcutta*. The editing of the second edition was the work of John Macfarlane, late librarian of the Imperial Library at Calcutta, and includes introductory notes by two eminent scholars of the early 1900s, H E A Cotton and G F Barwick, Superintendent of the British Museum Reading Room. Barwick summed up the educated guesses of his day: in spite of all the verifiable allusions, it had not been possible to identify an actual

'Sophia Goldborne' in the limited official circle in which she claims to have moved. Was it then a 'literary man', a hack, working at second-hand in England? Macfarlane, who had given a long time to its study, finally concluded that the book was 'the work of a lady'. Nearly a hundred years later Basham postulates another candidate, an elderly retired civilian, whose memory was becoming defective but who had written on hindu culture himself. 'Literary transvestism was very well known in England at the time.'[5] He also feels that passages on the East India Company, in their current aggressive warfare against the equally aggressive Maratta Confederacy 'might be taken to suggest that the author of *Hartly House* was in fact a man, for in the eighteenth century few women took any interest in politics'.[6] Seeing such eminent pundits disagree I will put forward another candidate, or rather two hypothetical candidates, equally impossible to verify. One point on which there can be no disagreement is that there are a number of inaccuracies: of distances, of easily verifiable facts; most striking of all are the inaccurate or approximate quotations. There is only accurate quotation from Thomson's *Seasons*, from 'Summer'. There are also the rather abrupt transitions from Sophia's arch style to her informative mode. I think *Hartly House* might prove to be the joint work, perhaps, of a young couple recently married, who wile away the long tedium of a voyage back from Bengal with the concoction of a wholly fictitious romance. And the only book they have an board is the indispensable Thomson. I consider a writing partnership accounts for the uneven leaps from topic to topic; further, the main hand was a woman's, for it is a woman's view of Calcutta, and the eye of an intelligent visitor not a long-time resident. 'Sophia' or her shadowy author might, had she stayed in Bengal, have matured into someone like the endearing matron, Lady Fanny Park,[7] who later published two rambling and well-informed volumes about her twenty-four years' stay in India. But Sophia did not stay long enough. A man alone would have found it hard to resist more details of the masculine world of Calcutta which memoirs of, say, William Hickey or Philip Francis, or the letters of Warren Hastings have since made familiar to us, a world only reflected at second hand in this novel. A man too might have urged restraint on giving too many possibly identifiable details about the hero, Doyly. A later Charles D'Oyly was the artist of the illustrated book already mentioned, *The European In India*,[8] and there were many of his family in the Indian Civil Service. There is not a shred of evidence to connect any of them with this novel. It should also be noted that the book was published in London just as Warren Hastings' impeachment for misconduct had suddenly brought Indian affairs into prominence. Was the novel part of the brisk partisan warfare that the Hastings affair caused; more subtle than a pamphlet and reaching a wider public? Again, there seems no evidence, though this possibility gives more weight to Basham's theory of the retired gentleman author. I prefer the shipboard scribblers, who may have found the novel worth publishing when Calcutta suddenly acquired news-value.

Sophia is a child of her age: silly enough, with her admirers, her vanity and her mistakes over her father's remarriage; sensitive enough to recognise and love the spare habits and austere elegance of mind of her Bramin; conventional enough to be ready to settle for Mr Doyly and his fortune and his agreeably oriental-ised behaviour; sentimental enough to have a mourning locket made from the hair of the dead Bramin. She had verve.

It is impossible for me not to believe in the identity of the young English girl who writes 'I adore the customs of the East' and goes on to describe a phaeton drive through the town, at the beginning of her visit, at the start of the Cold Weather of 1784, taking advan-tage of a cool breeze ...

Notes

1. A L Basham, 'Sophia and the "Bramin"' in K Ballhatchet and J Harrison (eds), *East India Company Studies*, London and Hong Kong, 1987, pp 13–30.

2. G Moorhouse, *Calcutta*, London, 1971, p 37.

3. Hastings, quoted by Philip Woodruff, *The Men Who Ruled India*, vol 1, *The Founders*, London, 1953, pp 124–5.

4. H E Busteed, *Echoes From Old Calcutta*, Calcutta, 1882.

5. Basham, p 25.

6. Basham, p 15.

7. F Park, *Wanderings of a Pilgrim in search of the Picturesque during four and twenty years in the East*, 2 vols, London, 1850.

8. C D'Oyly (artist) and T Williamson (text), *The European in India*, London, 1813.

INTRODUCTION TO THE
1908 EDITION.

It is remarkable that, in spite of researches extending over many years made by the late Mr. John Macfarlane, Librarian of the Imperial Library, Calcutta, the author of "Hartly House" still remains undiscovered. Although it is apparently written by a lady, moving in a limited official circle, who fills her book with allusions to her personal surroundings, it is nevertheless quite impossible to identify her. And yet the book attracted considerable attention at the time of publication. It was favourably noticed in the "Monthly Review" (1790, p. 332), and Mr. Macfarlane, in a letter to me of 7th June, 1906, spoke of the "considerable number of notices" of it which he had unearthed. An edition was issued in Dublin in the same year as the London one (1789), and a German translation was published at Leipzig two years later. The ordinary sources from which the author of an anonymous work is often discovered, such as private correspondence, presentation copies duly signed, or in a known handwriting, have all, so far, refused to give up the secret.

But whoever may have been the author,—whether the young lady we have supposed, or the literary man deriving his information at secondhand, and putting in the full complement of quotations from the poets, in accordance with the fashion of the day,—it is certain that "Hartly House" is a very remarkable book, and throws a flood of light upon Anglo-Indian society at one of the most interesting periods of the history of the Indian Empire. In view of one or two curious errors in regard to native customs Mr. Macfarlane was at one time disposed to regard the book as possibly a piece of hack work, but further consideration led him to give up that opinion entirely, and to recognise that it is the work of a lady, who wrote it a year or two after her return to England, and drew upon her recollections, and in a few instances, upon her imagination.

The large number of people who still take a keen interest in the career of Warren Hastings, will welcome a new edition of a book, which so vividly portrays the surroundings amid which he moved, and which so well illustrates his charming Letters to his wife, recently published by Miss Gregg ("Sydney C. Grier"). The original London edition, in three neat little volumes, and the Dublin reprint, are both so rare as to be almost unfindable, outside two or three great libraries.

I can only in conclusion express my regret that my late colleague and friend did not live to edit this book, and to give, with abler pen, the results of his researches in his own words.

G. F. BARWICK.

HARTLY HOUSE.

LETTER I.

THE grave of thousands!—Doubtless, my
good girl, in the successive years of European
visitation, the eastern world *is*, as you pronounce it, the grave of thousands; but is it
not also a mine of exhaustless wealth! the
centre of unimaginable magnificence! an
ever-blooming, an ever-brilliant scene? And
moreover, I have to inform you, that all the
prejudices you have so long cherished against
it must be done away; and for this plain reason, that they are totally groundless. Yes,
Arabella, the mother I have lost, and your
much so lamented friend, fell not, as we have
conceived, a victim to this ardent climate;
her pulse was not suspended by exotic disease;

I

the arrow of death was lodged in her gentle bosom *before* she left her native country, and she alone debarked, to expire on this coast. But take the melancholy fact, as my father was drawn out to relate it, during our voyage.

That the marriage of those to whom I am indebted for my existence was a marriage of affection, sanctified nevertheless by the approving voice of their parental relatives, is a circumstance you are well acquainted with; but, perhaps, it may be as new intelligence to you as it was to me, that from the tender distress mutually experienced on their first separation, in consequence of my father's profession, they resolved, on their re-union, never to separate more.

My birth gave them, however, a different turn of sentiment, though it in no degree lessened their conjugal attachment; my infant period being an insurmountable impediment to my mother's making an East India voyage, and my education a claim upon their feelings not to be dispensed with, until their confidence in the good understanding and excellent principles of your aunt at length persuaded them, their personal superintendence might, for a time at least, be safely intermitted;

then the firmness with which my mother bade me adieu, astonished all who knew her.

The India fleet was detained in the Channel by adverse winds; and in an excursion to Portsmouth, my mother caught a cold, which terminated in a cough. Yet did the extreme delicacy of her complexion, and uncomplaining turn of temper, prevent the discovery of a consumptive tendency, until it was too late to try the efficacy of softer climates than are to be met with in an East India voyage. She laboured, suffering angel as she was to give her husband hope, even when she herself despaired; talked, in the most touching terms, of the treasure they had left in England; and when the pious fraud could no longer be kept up, died, conjuring him to live for my sake. But I will not dwell upon so heart-wounding a subject · I indeed cannot, Arabella, for it has unhinged me, and I must quit my pen for a few moments.

If the packet I sent you from St. Helena (which was the first opportunity that offered) was put safely into your hands, or rather, if I could be assured that was the case, I might spare myself the trouble of accounting to you

for what you call my wonderful departure
from my native country ; an epithet that surprises me not, when I recollect the incoherence
and agitation with which I told the story of
my approaching embarkation ; but as I
must remain for months uncertain whether
it reached you or not, I will, on this occasion,
give you the particulars of my motives and
consequential conduct ; for I love you too
well to suffer you to suppose caprice, or the
wild curiosity of seeing foreign sights had any
share in my instantaneous resolution to visit
the eastern continent.

Having attended my father, as you well
know, to Deal, in order that we might enjoy
each other's company to the last possible
moment, I found, Arabella, on every renewed
good-night we exchanged, irrepressible sighs
escaped him.

The wind began to waver, and was expected
to come round to the favourable point before
the next morning's dawn I was retiring,
and the final farewell appeared to tremble on
my father's lips ; again I approached, and
again, to embrace him. My manner unspeakably affected him. It was nature's work ;
and when did nature ever work in vain ?

He held me for a short space, with silent anguish, in his arms, and I could alone articulate, " My father !—my dearest father ! " "Alas ! Sophia, " said he at length, "are my feelings prophetic ; shall I never more behold thee ? " " Oh, Sir ! " cried I, " revoke, I conjure you, your own decree ; nor be so cruel to yourself, when it is my anxious wish to accompany you, as to leave me behind. "

He lifted up his eyes and hands ; but made no reply.

I dropped instinctively on one knee before him. " My dearest Sir," resumed I, "if you persist in refusing my request and I live not to welcome your return to England, can you charge the calamity on aught but your own fiat ; for it is you, not Heaven, that forbids my sharing your destiny ; or, should I survive you, do not flatter yourself the tidings of your dissolution could be supported by me ; for who could convince me my presence might not have been soothing, or enable me to believe that somewhat of my suggesting might not have been salutary and prolonged your most-valued life ?—Your heart relents (perceiving I had subdued his resolves) ; I read it in your countenance ; and I take upon me, short soever as the time may prove, to be prepared to go with you." He laid his pocket-book open on the table, bad me use the contents without reserve, and, to hide his emotion, hastily retired.

With what alacrity and expedition I provided the necessaries for my voyage I need not mention; for who has not heard of the all-creative power of gold, and the rapid movement of the wings of inclination?

We embarked together and have, without one alarming (that is unusual) incident, made the Bay of Bengal. This letter shall therefore be constituted the repository of a private vow I have entered into with myself, never to marry in Indostan, lest it should become difficult, at some future period, to ascertain my genuine impulse for quitting the country of my birth; a vow, take notice, Arabella, I will not violate to be a nabobess.

And thus concludes my last epistle, unanimated by oriental suns, and unperfumed by oriental breezes. An indescribable degree of vivacity already diffuses itself through my heart, insomuch that I hasten to tell you, in the cold language of European friendship

(before I blush to have known its frigid influence) that I am your's affectionately,

SOPHIA GOLDBORNE.

LETTER II.

Hartly House, Calcutta.

THE splendour of this house, as it is modestly styled, is of itself, my Arabella, sufficient
to turn the soundest European head ; but I
am well aware, was I to plunge at once into
a description of it, I should have my veracity,
if not my intellects, impeached ; lowering myself, therefore, to your narrow conceptions, I
will begin with the circumstances of my first
arrival, and so contrive to temper, though I
cannot, like Mr. Apollo, lay aside my rays,
that your optics shall be enabled to contem-
plate, however brilliant, the dazzling objects
I gradually open on your view.

The Island of Sawger, at the mouth of the
Ganges, is the first land you encounter ; but as
it is alone inhabited by tigers, alligators, &c.,
&c., you will believe me when I tell you I had
not the smallest *penchant* for visiting it.

Pilots, however, come down to this distance (some hundred miles) from Calcutta, for the safe convoy of ships ; the tide of this eastern river being subject to no less sudden than impetuous changes, insomuch that the ablest seamen are often drifted by it.

We proceeded on our voyage up the river to one of the stations for Indiamen, called Culpee, 150 miles from Calcutta, where my father received the most affectionate greetings from his old acquaintance ; and we were told, that three *bugeros* were on their way to welcome and accommodate us.

This sound having no semblance whatever of the eastern dignity, I begged my father to inform me what a *bugero* was :—He smiled and bid me wait their arrival, nor seek to anticipate my own discoveries in a single instance.

We next passed the second station called Cudgeree ; when lo, the *bugeros* appeared in view ; and judge, if you can, of the pleasure it gave me, after having been so long confined to one set of company, to perceive I was on the point of tasting the boundless joys of eastern magnificence.

You have seen, as you suppose, some very handsome barges on the river Thames ; but

how poor a figure the handsomest would
make, in comparison with the *bugeros*, or
barges of Calcutta, I will endeavour to convince you.

As they approached, my ears drank in the
most delightful sounds ; a band of music, as is
the custom, occupied each of them, playing the softest airs ; and from the *tout en-
semble*, brought Dryden's Cydnus and Cleo-
patra to my recollection.

The company in the first that came along-
side of us were seated upon deck, with kittesan boys, in the act of suspending their kitte-
sans, * which were finely ornamented, over
their heads ; which boys were dressed in white
muslin jackets, tied round the waist with
green sashes, and gartered at the knees in
like manner with the puckered sleeves in
England, with white turbans bound by the
same coloured ribband ; the rowers, resting
on their oars in a similar uniform, made a
most picturesque appearance.

My foolish heart was in the *bugero*, before
my father, at the earnest solicitations of his
friends, and a look of desire from me, assisted

* Umbrellas.

me to descend from the ship ; but, when des-
cended, my astonishment and delight so abundantly increased at each advanced step, that
the European world faded before my eyes,
and became *orientalised* at all points.

Eight gentlemen, three of whom were my
father's particular friends, and four ladies,
were the party, and it appears to me, Arabella, that I shall find every poetical description realised in this enchanting quarter of the
globe ; for be it known to you, in the language
of Southern's Oroonoko, that when presented
to the gentlemen as my father's daughter, I
bowed, and *blushed* ; and, if I have any skill
in physiognomy, they *wondered* and *adored* ;
and such, I already understand, is the court
paid to ladies at Calcutta, that it would be
well worth any vain woman's while, who has
a tolerable person, to make the voyage I have
done, in order to enjoy unbounded homage.

The chief article of refreshment was claret,
which was drank with great freedom, under
the name of *Loll Shrub*. Coffee, tea, sweet-
meats, etc., etc., were offered, but in general
refused, except by my father, who is fond of
coffee to a degree that I think will not accord
with his health in this relaxing climate.

A kittesan boy instantly took his stand behind my chair, and an attendant, called a bearer, flew backwards and forwards in my service ; and in this state we reached Diamond Point, a place of debarkation, where we found a suitable number of palanquins in waiting to accommodate us all.

I was startled, Arabella, however prepared, on finding myself hoisted on the men's shoulders ; for I need not observe to you, the only difference between a palanquin and a London sedan-chair (except the travelling ones) is their having short poles fastened to the central part of the sides, the front pair of which have a curve for the bearer's better hold —venetian-blinds instead of glass windows— and in the mode of carrying.

It was evening ; I therefore, as well as my father, and the rest of the company, had two har-carriers, or flambeaux-bearers, running before me ; and I felt all the dignity of my transition ; though I will confess to you, the *Tok, Tok*, their almost perpetual cry, to clear the way, did not fall so agreeable on my ear as I could have wished ; nor was I able to suppress the invocation of *auri veni* at every footstep,

From the point where we landed, to the Esplanade (a place I shall describe to you on
my own acquaintance with it) is almost four
miles ; and swiftly did we pass along ; for it
seems the palanquin-bearers (with proper
relays, as is the case with those that perform
journies) are so expert that in defiance of the
heat, etc., etc., they go at the rate of from nine
to twelve miles an hour.

I could only observe by the light of the
flambeaux (though a host of servants poured
forth to receive us) that the entrance to Hartly House was by means of a double flight of
stone steps, at the top of which we found a
spacious balcony called a veranda, covered
in by venetian-blinds, and lighted up with
wax candles, placed under glass shades, to
prevent their extinction from the free admission of the evening breeze ; together with
a couple of card-tables, furnished at all points,
for those disposed to occupy them, with very
many other polite *et cœtera's*.

Here I met with homage, in the form of
congratulation's on my safe arrival ; but re-
collecting it would not be to forfeit it in future, if I declined it at the then moment, I
complained of fatigue, and was conducted to

an apartment that would have satisfied a princess, though neither more nor less than a common genteel sleeping-room.

The furniture was all Chinese, of the elegant materials and manufacture of which, even you people in England have a very tolerable idea; but the vases and the perfumes were superior to everything of the kind within my knowledge, and as such had a fine effect on my feelings.

My musketto curtains are made of beautiful muslin, extremely full, and capable of considerable expansion; and it is the custom for the servants to beat them immediately before going to bed, to clear them of those insects; when they are just sufficiently opened to admit the party, and suddenly closed to exclude those troublesome nocturnal companions; then, being spread out wide, they admit the air in the most refreshing degree. Apropos of muskettos; I must tell you, though I shudder at the bare recollection of so vulgar a nuisance, that, in like manner with the bugs in London, they mercilessly annoy all newcomers, blistering them, and teazing, if not torturing them continually; and in a great measure spare those who are seasoned to the climate.

And now let me ask you your opinion of
my attachment to you, when I can thus forego the highest earthly pleasures, flattery and
luxurious accommodation, for your amusement. But perhaps, instead of thinking
yourself obliged to me, you will, with the true
European *sangfroid*, suspect me of self-grati-
fication in my descriptions ;—beware, however, of such erroneous conclusions, as you
value the future favours of your own

SOPHIA GOLDBORNE.

P. S.—We are, they tell me (yet such is the
present warmth that, without the information,
I should not have supposed it) arrived at the
commencement of the temperate season, and
I am taught to expect a very fine climate for
five successive months, the monsoons not coming on until February, when agues and fevers
are epidemic ; and my constitution, no doubt,
Arabella, must undergo its naturalization ; for
few indeed are the exceptions to these several
attacks, which often lead down to final dissolution. The idea shakes my constancy !
Oh ! pray devoutly with me, that my dearest
father may be spared in his own health, and
unwounded in mine ; for well do I know he
could depart in peace, if his child was not to

be left behind. And to survive her!—Can any thought be more killing? Good-night —I will try to lose it, and all my cares in that sweet balm of our existence, sleep. Once more, therefore, good-night!

LETTER III.

————— —————Prime cheerer! Light,
Of all created beings first and best!
Efflux divine!

IT is morn, you must understand, Arabella, with us sons and daughters of the East, six hours at least before you enjoy the glorious, however, weakened sun-beams; and I awoke to encounter new wonders.

Having breakfasted, (which I find is the only *dégagé* meal I must hope to enjoy, every one ordering what is most agreeable to their choice, and in elegant undress chatting *á la volonté;* whilst, on the contrary, dinner, tea, and supper are kind of state levees) knowing that in the next apartment to mine, a *country-born* young lady—as the phrase is to distinguish them from Europeans—was lodged, whom I had found extremely winning in

her address during our voyage in the *bugero*,
and declaredly ambitious to be admitted on
the list of my friends ; I took it in my head to
visit her *en passant*, and make her a morning compliment ; and this the more particularly, because she had not given us her company
at breakfast, and I imagined she might have
taken cold on the water. But judge my
surprise, Arabella, when, on entering her
chamber, I found her under the hands of her
hair-dresser, actually smoking a pipe.

But let me caution you against every plebeian idea on the occasion, for that pipe was
a most superb *hooka*, the bell filled with rose-
water ; and instead of odious tobacco, a preparation of the betel-root, rolled up, and wet-
ted, was placed in the bole, which bole was
beautiful china-ware, covered with a filligree
silver cap, with a mouthpiece of the same
materials. Nor can I give you a conception of
the graceful manner in which the snake (the
long ornamented tube) was twined through
the rails of her chair, and turned under her
arm, so as not to have incommoded any person
seated by her ; or the genteel air with which
she drew out the soft fume, and puffed it
forth, alternately (for none of it is retained).

In a word I wished to have taken her portrait
on the spot, for her form is elegant, her complexion near the European standard, and the
novelty of her attitude such, as rendered them
altogether an admirable subject for the pencil.

This kind of smoking is, I am told, the
characteristic custom of the *country-born*
ladies ; and the servant, dressed as I have already described, whose sole business it is to
arrange the snake, feed the fire on his knees,
and take care of the whole apparatus, is called
the hooka-bearer, and is an indispensable ap-
pendage of Eastern state and etiquette. The
gentlemen, without distinction, indulge themselves this way, and as naturally, I am informed, fill up the period of their hair-dressing
with their hookas, as those in England with
perusing the daily prints, and unquestionably
to a more beneficial purpose ; for the health
is preserved or promoted by the practice :
whereas news-paper reading, in your fashionable world, only furnishes the head with politics, and the heart with scandal, no very estimable acquisition, I hope you will grant me,
for a rational member of the community.

I have this morning enabled myself to give
you some idea of the houses at Calcutta—

H. H.   2

for all of them, of any consequence, are, I am
assured, built upon a similar plan, though not
all with similar advantages of situation.
To begin with

HARTLY MANSION.

The centre part of the building is much
higher than the rest, and terminates in a
point at the top, forming an obtuse angle (if
I may properly so call it) when the projecting
lines are downwards, and extend to the wings
on each side ; the roof whereof covers a most
magnificent hall, or saloon, the whole length
and breadth of this central space ornamented
at both fronts with balconies, or verandas,
that open by folding glass-doors of inconceiv-
able grandeur, into the above mentioned apartment ; and the architecture, having the advantage of every possible decoration, (together
with large-sized windows over the balconies)
has a striking effect on an European beholder.

From this grand centre the wings project,
each of which consists of a suite of elegant
rooms, all on one floor—(for the utmost ele-
vation from the ground is the flight of steps
at the entrance) with a view of the Esplanade
in front, a kind of immense park ; and a

large garden, with a fine tank or fish-pond behind—such as sleeping rooms, dressing-rooms, with drawing-rooms, etc., etc., in a style, no set of words I am mistress of can convey to your imagination ;—and under this prodigious structure are the family offices in general ; the exceptions are store-houses with the offices, at a distance, instead of gardens. The hall is, it seems, on all occasions, the place where dinner and supper are served up ; and, when illuminated, as the lustres and girandoles bespeak, must be fit for the reception of a royal guest.

The outside of the walls is washed with a white composition called *chinam*, that, in like manner with the scenes in your theatres, has no glare, and of course is not painful (how powerful soever the sun's rays may be) to the sight ; which *chinam* is a pleasing contrast to the lively green of the verandas, or venetian blinds, universally used, whether the windows are glass or not), and are reliefs to each other, but glass, you must know, is a dear commodity at Calcutta, and imported solely from England ; on which account the governor's house is almost the only one that can boast that distinction.

The venetian blinds (or *verandas*, as I shall accustom you to call them) answer two most desirable purposes—shade, and the free current of air, without which there would be no existing—Eastern pomp, splendor, and magnificence, support me in this trying moment ! when, almost expiring with heat, (and the seldom heard of, in Europe, misery of laboured respiration) I am on the point of confessing, no happiness can equal the happiness of a temperate climate, and the social intercourse of the sons and daughters of Liberty and intellectual cultivation ; for, my dear Arabella, too true it is, that the best pleasure of the East is, being a kind of state-prisoner, enfeebled and fettered by vertical suns, and the fatigue of veiling our distresses from vulgar optics, by gaudy trappings and the pomp of retinue ; nor can I suppose it possible, I should ever become habituated to what I now languish under, and cease to sigh for one delightful strole in St. James' Park, unincumbered by palanquins, kittesan-bearers, the clamour of har-carriers, etc., etc.

I reprobate all I have written.—My father has this instant filled my purse with gold mohrs value forty shillings, or sixteen rupees each ;

has purchased me a palanquin (what prophana-
tion have I not been guilty of against palanquins!) and my mind is restored to the pin-
nacle of grandeur, from which it had so meanly
fallen.—I am nevertheless, in despite of myself,

Yours, as usual,

S. G.

———

LETTER IV.

'Tis raging noon, and vertical the sun
Darts on the head direct its forceful beams ;
O'er heaven and earth, far as the ranging eye
Can sweep, a dazzling deluge reigns.

THOMPSON certainly passed a part of his
life under this meridian, so applicable are the
above lines to my present situation. You
cannot therefore wonder, if you give them an
attentive perusal, at the weakness into which
I was surprised at the conclusion of my last
letter, or that the poet's words,

All conquering heat ! O intermit thy wrath,
And on my throbbing temples potent thus
Beam not so fierce.

should at this moment spontaneously flow
from my pen. But we will talk no more of it.

The royal levee was never more crowded
than mine—fine fellows, Arabella, without
number ! —the East India Company's servants ! the English sovereign's servants !—
I trust I shall not dwindle again into my
former self, or yawn away my days under your
gloomy atmosphere. But I wander wide
from my intended subject.

I have been at Church, my dear girl, in my
new palanquin, (the mode of genteel-convey-
ance) where *all* ladies are approached, by sanction of ancient custom, by *all* gentlemen in-
discriminately, known or unknown, with offers
of their hand to conduct them to their seat ;
accordingly those gentlemen who wish to
change their condition (which, between ourselves, are chiefly old fellows, for the young
ones either chuse country-born ladies for
wealth or having left their hearts behind them,
enrich themselves in order to be united to their
favourite Dulcineas in their native land) on
hearing of a ship's arrival, make a point of
repairing to this holy dome and eagerly tender their services to the fair strangers ; who,
if this stolen view happens to captivate, often,
without undergoing the ceremony of a formal
introduction, receive matrimonial overtures

and, becoming brides in the utmost possible splendor, have their rank instantaneously established, and are visited, and paid every honour to which the consequence of their husbands entitles them. But not so your friend; for, having accompanied my father to India, no overtures of that nature will be attempted, previous to an acquaintance with him, or at least under his encouraging auspices; nor did any gentleman break in upon the circle of my surrounding intimates, on this first public exhibition of my person, though every male creature in Calcutta, entitled to that privilege, bid Mr. and Mrs. Hartly expect an early visit from them. On my mentioning the church, you will perhaps fancy I ought to recount to you its magnificence and style of architecture; but the edifice dignified at present with that appellation does not deserve notice. It is situated at the Old Fort, and consists solely of a ground-floor, with an arrangement of plain pews; nor is the Governor himself much better accommodated than the rest; and of course the Padra, as the clergymen is called, has little to boast of; the windows are, however, verandas, which are pleasing to me in their appearance, independent of the blessing

of air enjoyed through that medium. But
at the New Fort there is a new church erect-
ing, on quite an European model, with gal-
leries, a set of bells, and every suitable *et
cætera* ; the plan and foundation of which,
have seen, conversed with the architect, and,
from the whole, form very high expectations
of the superstructure. One remark, however
is a-propos on this subject ; namely, that the
house of prayer, at Calcutta, is not the house
of sepulchre. Burying-grounds are provided
some miles from the town, which I am given
to understand, are well worth the visit of a
stranger. I will only add, that though this
measure may have arisen from the fervid
heat of this climate (where death is busy)
which gives the idea of rapid putridity, yet
surely it is disgracing the temple of the Divinity (admitting even that in England no bad
consequence results from such deposits), to
make it a charnel-house.—Let this suffice for
churches, except the mention that at Calcutta
Sunday is the only day of public devotion and
that only in the morning ; though the Padra's
salary is liberal, and his perquisites immense.

Think you, Arabella, that on mentioning
the awful repositories of the dead, I forget

my dear mother's sacred remains? —Surely
no. But I wish not to hang unnecessary
weights on your spirits, and therefore reserve
all I have to say on that heart-searching subject, for the period that enables me to tell you,
I have beheld her hallowed tomb, and paid
the best tribute in my poor power to her beloved memory! Adieu! adieu!—I will resume my pen the first opportunity ; but can
no more at present.

S. G.

LETTER V.

You would, my Arabella, be enraptured at
the extreme neatness of even the meanest
attendant ; but besides the beauty and the
virtue of cleanliness, it is the only fence in the
·East against putrid diseases. That unerring
guide, Nature, who teaches the people of the
North to fortify themselves with furs against
their inclement seasons, bids the inhabitants
of Indostan be correctly delicate in their persons, and personal attire : to which the circumstance of all the servants being Gentoos

not a little contributes ; for diurnal immersion
in the river Ganges is one of the strict articles
of their religion, at the same time that it is a
general benefit to the Europeans.

The Moors, or Mahometans, and the Gentoos,
compose the chief body of the public ; but
perhaps, Arabella, you may wish and expect
I should present you with some account of the
ancient inhabitants of this astonishing empire,
before I introduce you to an acquaintance with
the moderns as the living generations may
possibly be deemed by you. You must, however, excuse me ; historical anecdotes are not
compatible with either the taste or leisure of a
fine lady at Bengal. I will indeed advance
so far on this heavy ground in your service,
as to inform you where you may meet with
such matter of fact, and spare myself the drudg-
ery, as well as the disgrace, of exercising my
pen thereon. Yet, when I turn my thoughts
that way, I must believe it will cost me less
labour to write the little it is necessary for you
to read, than to refer you to the chapter and
verse of those authors who have treated of
this world of wonders ; for, in the first place,
Arabella, take notice, the work of creation was
performed in the East, and in the East Chris-

tianity received its birth ; in consequence of
which great circumstances, the sublime ideas
and discoveries perpetually opening themselves upon my mind, can alone be even faintly
conceived by you, if you, (as I recommend it to
you to do) travel over so highly-distinguished
a region, traced out as it is on your globes,
with the sacred and prophane writers of anti-
quity in your hand—when your entertainment
will be ample.   I speak from experience.   The
other particulars run thus :—

India, it is supposed, was first peopled from
Persia, (which, in conjunction with the Indian
ocean, is its western boundary) because, by
its contiguity to that kingdom, it lies in the
way of Mesopotamia, where, it is generally
agreed, the descendants of Noah settled after
the deluge.   Be this as it may, it is evidently
the southern division, (for there is not a white
man, or any complexion but black, amongst
its numerous inhabitants) and was possessed
by the Ethiopians : their colour, long hair
and regular features being markingly different
from the blacks of Guinea ; and, as a further
proof of their Ethiopian origin, we read in
our Bible, that the queen of Sheba (which
Sheba is only another name for Ethiopia) sent

presents to the wise king Solomon, of many
spices—which alone grow in India, and were
brought thither from Ethiopia for cultivation.

The next people who possessed the country
were Arabians ; for certain it is that almost the
whole coast was subject to Arabian or Mahometan princes, when the Portuguese arrived
there in 1500 ; which Arabs, there is held little
doubt, dispossessed the Ethiopians of their
territories, and drove them up into the midland country, which they still inhabit.

The next invaders were the Mogul Tartars
under Tamerlane, about the year 1400, who
fixed his third son in the North of India and
Persia ; but the southern provinces were not
reduced under the dominion of the Mogul,
until the reign of Aurengzebe, in 1667. This
prince, it seems, had been shown some of the
large diamonds from the mines of Golconda
(the grand magnet at this day), and was thence
induced to attempt the conquest thereof ; and
a good substantial motive it was ; whereas
the mighty Alexander overspread the universe with his armies, for the sole purpose of
restoring, in the form of a generous act, those
kingdoms his superior force wrested from their
lawful and peaceful possessors. But to return

to Aurengzebe. He made himself at length
master of all the country as far as Cape
Comorin, which, if you look in your map,
you will find to be the most southern pro-
montory of India ; but the midland country
being very mountainous and woody and subject moreover to several Ethiopian princes
called Rajahs, preserved, by their united
efforts, their independence ; insomuch, that
they alone acknowledge the Mogul for their
sovereign at the present period in instances
you will meet with hereafter.

In the time of the famous Persian monarch,
Khouli Khan, the Mogul throne was possessed
by a great grandson of Aurengzebe, who was
made prisoner by that bold and enterprising
Persian, and obliged to cede him all the North-
west provinces of India to obtain his liberty.
This invasion cost the poor Gentoos two hundred thousand lives. As to the plunder made
by Khouli Khan, well authenticated accounts
speak it to be no less than two hundred and
thirty millions sterling ; his own private share
of which was considerably above seventy millions, and may be considered as terminat-
ing the greatness of the Mogul empire in the
house of Tamerlane : nevertheless, when he

had raised all the money he could in Delhi,
he reinstated the Mogul Mahomed Shah in
the sovereignty, and returned to his own
country.

A general defection of the provinces ensued,
none being willing to yield obedience to a
prince deprived of the power of enforcing it.
The provinces ceded to Khouli Khan were
only a short time enjoyed by him ; for in 1747,
he was assassinated ; and Achmet Abdallah,
his treasurer, equally unprincipled as his royal
master, being a man of great intrepidity,
found means, in the general confusion, to
carry off three hundred camels loaded with
wealth, and, putting himself at the head of
an army, marched against Delhi with fifty
thousand horse. Thus was the wealth, drawn
from this powerful city, made the instrument
of continuing the miseries of war, which it
had at first brought upon them. At present
the imperial dignity is vested, after manifold revolutions, in a prince that is universally acknowledged to be the true heir
of the Tamerlane race ; but his power is
feeble, the city of Delhi, and a small territory round it, being all that is left re-
maining to that ancient and magnificent

house ; and he depends upon the protection of the English, whose interest it is to support him, as his authority is the best legal guarantee.

The point of prudence, however, in the East India Company is, that their Governors should interfere as little as possible in the domestic or national quarrels of the country powers ; peace and tranquility best promoting their commercial interests. The wars with the Marattas, and Prince Hyderally, indeed, prove that these maxims have not always been properly adhered to. But I do not intend to pass myself off for a politician ; and, therefore, leaving these modern particulars undiscussed, affirm, that this is historical knowledge sufficient for any reasonable woman, who is in the way of receiving more extensive intelligence from incidental observation and hourly occurrences. But I must beseech you to keep these matters distinct in your head, that you may comprehend, on the instant, the references or elucidations I may present you with.

You will marvel at my reading and literary talents ; but please to remember, that we alone know our depth of information or abil-

ities, when occasion calls them forth.—I need
not say how much I am,

Your's
S. G.

LETTER VI.

THIS, Arabella, shall be a long letter ; for
it shall contain an account of one whole day,
spent after the Calcutta manner ; which, I
conceive, will prove so close a copy of the
general mode of living, that little more will
be left for me to say on that subject ; for the
variations in amusement, exercise, etc., etc.,
cannot be considerable, in a place, where, to
render existence supportable, is the sole end
and purpose of elegance, as well as of industry.

At nine o'clock it is the custom of this family to breakfast ; and I, who am no daughter of
solitude, so soon as it is announced, become
visible ; for I have much pleasure in Mrs.
Hartly's conversation.

The fashionable undress, except in the
article of being without stays (and stays are

wholly unworn in the East) is much in the English style, with large caps, or otherwise, as fancy dictates : it is however, sufficient to say, no care or skill is left unexerted to render the appearance easy and graceful—a rather necessary circumstance, as you will grant me, when I add, that the gentlemen, in the course of their morning excursions (for they ride out on horseback at an early hour) continually drop in ; and, from the numerous acquaintances this house can boast, I apprehend we shall seldom know a breakfast unaccompanied by these casual visitants—who say the prettiest things imaginable, with an air of truth that wins on the credulity, and harmonizes the heart. Not, Arabella, but a fine woman, robed in white muslin, and with every other species of attractive drapery (let me tell you) is a very striking object ; and, as such, honestly entitled to admiration.

You probably conceive, that, in this gay and enervating climate, industry is the last idea that would suggest itself to the mind of a fine lady : but you are mistaken ; for the ladies at Calcutta are very fond of working upon muslin, of knotting, netting, and all the

little methods of whiling away the time, without hanging weights on the attention.

At twelve a repast is introduced, consisting
of cold ham, chickens, and loll shrub ; after
partaking of which, all parties separate to dress.

The friseur now forms the person anew ;
and those who do not chuse to wear caps, however elegant or ornamented, have flowers of
British manufacture (a favourite mode of decoration) intermixed with their tresses, and
otherwise disposed so as to have an agreeable
effect. Powder is, however, used in great
quantities, on the idea of both coolness and
neatness ; though, in my opinion, the natural
colour of the hair would be more becoming :
but the intense heat, I suppose, renders it
ineligible.

At three the day after my arrival, as is
usually the case, the company assembled in
the hall or saloon, to the number of four-and-
twenty ; where, besides the lustres and girandoles already mentioned, are sofas of Chinese
magnificence : but they are only substituted
for chairs ; what is called lolling in the
western world, being here unpractised.

The dinner table was covered with snow-
white damask table-cloth of the finest tex-

ture; and to every plate were arranged two
glasses, one of a pyramidical and slender
form (like the hob-nob glasses in England)
for loll shrub, the other a common-sized wine-
glass, for whatever beverage is most agreeable ; and between every two persons at table
were also placed a decanter of water and a
tumbler, for diluting at pleasure ; with folded
napkins, of equal elegance with the table-cloth,
for all the company marked by art, with a
variety of fanciful figures, which I reluctantly
destroyed.

Such hosts of men on all occasions present
themselves, that, at dinner, to the demolition
of scandal and all other personal subjects, no
two ladies are permitted, I find, in this country, to sit by each other. But the sexes are
blended (I will not say in pairs, for the men are
out of all proportion to the female world) so
as to aid the purposes of gallantry and good
humour; and, during the whole period of
dinner, boys with flappers and fans surround
you, procuring at least a tolerably comfortable artificial atmosphere.

The dishes were so abundant, and the re-
moves so rapid, I can only tell you, ducks,
chickens, fish (no soup, take notice, is served

up at Calcutta) and all the *et cæteras* of an
English bill of fare, according to their proper
seasons, passed before my eyes.

But the mode of dressing these provisions is somewhat curious ; for, I am told, fires
of a particular kind of wood are prepared,
which being burnt to a clinker, the animal or
joint intended to be roasted is placed *over*
not *before* them ; where they are turned about
until done in the greatest perfection ; the fires
being so judiciously fed, as to prevent both
decay of heat, and smoke.

The attention and court paid to me was
astonishing ; my smile was meaning, and my
articulation melody : in a word, mirrors are
almost useless things at Calcutta, and self-
adoration idle ; for your looks are reflected
in the pleasure of the beholder, and your
claims to first-rate distinction confessed by
all who approach you.

After the circulation of a few loyal healths,
etc., etc., the ladies withdraw ; and the gentlemen, I am told, drink their chearful glass
for some time beyond that period, insomuch,
that it is no unfrequent thing for each man to
dispatch his three bottles of claret, or two of
white wine, before they break up ; having the

bottles so emptied piled up before them as
trophies of their prowess.

The ladies at Calcutta retire, not to enjoy
their private chat, or regret their separation
from their admirers ; for to sleep is the object
of their wishes, and the occupation of their
time—a refreshment that alone enables
them to appear with animation in the evening : accordingly both ladies and gentlemen
entirely undress, and repose on their beds, in
the same manner as at the midnight hour ;
and, on awaking, are a second time attended
by their hair-dresser ; and thus, a second time
in the twenty-four hours, come forth armed
at all points for conquest.

But it shall not be concealed, Arabella,
that so great an enemy to beauty is this ardent climate, that even I, your newly-arrived
friend, am only the ghost of my former self ;
and, however, the lily has survived, the roses
have expired : neither my lips (the glow of
which you yourself have noticed) or cheeks
are much more barely distinguishable from
the rest of my face, and that only by the
faintest bloom imaginable. Art, therefore,
is here (as well as in Britain) a substitute
for nature in ninety-nine instances out of a

hundred. I hope I miscalculate my countrywomen in this comparison ; but you know me
too well to suspect me of a departure from
my established custom. Notwithstanding all
which, from being a new figure at Calcutta,
my father's partiality for his only child (the
only child of a woman he adored) is gratified
beyond measure by the unending themes of
my celebrity—my dress, my address, my
judgment, my understanding, my language,
my sentiments, my taste. Fear with me
then, my good Arabella, that I have cut out
much distressing business for myself in the
refusing line, by the rash vow I registered and
transmitted you from Bengal Bay, and by
which I religiously conceive myself bound to
regulate my conduct.

I have slept little this morning. A whirl
of ideas I am unable to regulate, was the
cause. I am, however, dressed ; and my new
friend calls upon me to attend her to the tea-
room. I come, I come. She is gone without me, Arabella, from imagining me not ready
to present myself ; and I will borrow so much
time as just to describe the household retinue
of Mr. and Mrs. Hartly, and, of course, of all
the genteel families in Calcutta.

The ranks of natives from whence the domestic servants are obtained, are Gentoos (I think I told you as much in a former letter, but no matter, the repetition will only confirm my report) they do not board in the European families; but, receiving a weekly stipend (and that a very slender one) feed at their own hovels, on rice and fish, during the hours of their masters and mistresses reposing themselves, and then, with renewed alacrity, resume their several appointments and offices.

The suite of servants consists of a coachman and groom, which are generally Europeans; a consumer, who is a Gentoo (a kind of house steward and butler, for he provides every family article, and attends the side-board and tea-table in person, with bearers, all Gentoos, of several denominations; the chief of which is called the Seda-bearer, who cleans the tables, places the glass shades over the candles in the verandas, and has the care of his master's shoes, which he puts on and takes off for him with the profoundest respect); two pair of palanquin-bearers; a kittesan-bearer; two harcarriers, or flambeaux-bearers; a hooka-bearer; and the bearers who stand behind chairs, and act as waiters to and from the tea-table : and so diligent and discerning are they that they read the commands of the company in their eyes, and seem created for the sole purpose and sole ambition of serving the Europeans.

The muslin dresses, etc., etc., which I mentioned to you on the adventure of the bugeros are, it proves, the family liveries of the East ; I mean the colour of the sashes and turban ribbands ; my colour is the Tyrian dye, which I need not tell you, has a beautiful effect upon white.

I am sent for, and must for the present bid you adieu !

————

Three o'clock, morning.

You will, perhaps, Arabella, be so unbred as to conclude, some particular party or amusement has kept me up till this late hour ; but know, two is absolutely a plebeian time of breaking up company at Calcutta.—Refreshed by your afternoon's sleep, and braced by the cool breezes of the evening, you consider time as made only for enjoyment, and repose as an outrage on conviviality.

My new friend, the country-born lady, met me the day after my arrival, and led the way to the tea-party ; but instead of a parlour, etc., I found this party collected in the veranda, as on the preceding evening, and I drank my tea with a degree of satisfaction unknown in England in large companies ; for, Arabella, instead of the exchanges (a most alarming and disgusting idea) to which you are there exposed, it is the delightful and sensible custom at Calcutta, for a bearer to convey your cup, when empty, to the consumer, without once letting it go out of his hands ; and of course returns it you secure from every possibility of contamination.— I think—I never was so pleased with any one article of polite etiquette in my whole life.

At dinner we were cooled by artificial means ; but the heavenly breezes of evening reached us through the verandas—cheered, enlivened, and rendered us quite another order of beings.

Tea and coffee over, three card-tables (for sorry I am to tell you, card-playing is here, in like manner as in Europe, the fashionable propensity) were brought forward, and I, as a visiter, and a stranger, was not permitted to decline. I was on the point of seating myself, when the stake was mentioned ; but what was my astonishment, when I heard five gold mohrs (ten pounds) spoke of as a very moderate sum a corner !

I drew back, Arabella, instinctively ; for the little treasure my father had so kindly made me mistress of, my heart told me, at this rate, would literally make itself wings, and flee away.

Mrs. Hartly, perceiving both my surprise and chagrin, asked me to honour her table with my company, where, she said, they were so humble as to stake only poor one gold mohr —I gladly accepted her invitation ; and endeavoured to remember with fortitude, that forty good shillings sterling would either be won or lost by me in the course of a few deals ; whist being the polite game.

It is observed by some author, (but I do not immediately recollect who) that intoxication is the vice of a barbarous, gambling of a refined people ; this is verified to a fatal proverb in this spot ; for fortune, in the East (however refined the taste or manners of its possessor) appears alone to be acquired for the purpose of this wild dissipation of it ; insomuch, that the *ultimatum* of European desires, the return to their native country, is sacrificed to the gratification of this pernicious propensity, as well as the peace and felicity of many most deserving families. In a word, several hundred pounds were transferred from their possessors in the short period we were engaged.

At supper the saloon was superbly lighted, and the table sumptuously covered. The same ceremony of parting the ladies was observed, as I have already described ; so that the decanter and tumbler are evidently designed for her accommodation : and a band of music was introduced, which played all the evening.

I was requested to favour the company with a song (vocal music being highly esteemed by the *Calcutonians*) ; and so anxious were the gentlemen to discover whether I had a voice tuned to melody, or not, that doubt and expectation sat on each countenance.

I dispelled their doubts, and, if the goddess of Flattery (who certainly touched the lips of her votaries with peculiar eloquence on the occasion) may be relied on, exceeded all they could have hoped for from the first daughter of Harmony. It must, however, be seriously

acknowledged, that, from indolence, relaxed
fibres, or whatever other cause or impediment,
my little powers equalled the best efforts of
my fair friends ; and I have bound myself by
a solemn promise, to be an *angel* on each
succeeding evening.

A jingling of unaccustomed sounds to my
ears now interrupted my eulogiums, and immediately six or seven black girls were brought
in, dressed in white muslin, loaded with ribbands of various colours, with two or three
gold rings in their noses, by way of ornament,
and silver casnets at their ancles and wrists,
with which they beat time very agreeably to
the tamborines that attended them. These
are called *notch-girls*, (the word for dance)
and their performance is called *notchee*. They
sang lively and tender compositions alternately,
as was apparent by the movement of their
eyes and hands, but to me otherwise unintel-
ligible ; danced with good effect ; and, I could
perceive, were well rewarded. After which,
the night being particularly fine, we were
instantly conveyed in our palanquins to the
Company's gardens ; late in the evening, or
absolutely midnight, being the only walking
time in this climate. The moon was near the

full, and her silver beams displayed unusual lustre. Flowers of the most beautiful aspect and delightful scent, aromatic trees and shrubs ʹperfumed the breeze ; and the vistos, or shady walks, had an air of enchantment ! Thus was the evening terminated, or, more properly, Arabella, the new-born day welcomed with uxurious glee ; the senses flattered ; the heart softened ; and love and friendship the prevailing sensations of the soul !—For, where the mind is pure, under such auspices as I have described, love is friendship, and friendship affection.

You are now, my dear girl, thinking of your temperate and solitary supper ; and may a repose succeed, tranquil as your nature.

Adieu !

S. G.

LETTER VII.

BEAR me, Pomona! to thy Citron groves;
To where the Lemon and the piercing Lime,
With the deep Orange, glowing thro' the green,
Their lighter glories blend: lay me reclin'd
Beneath the spreading Tamarind, that shakes,
Fann'd by the breeze, its fever-cooling fruit :
Deep in the night the massy Locust sheds,
Quench my hot limbs : or lead me thro' the maze
Embowering endless, of the Indian Fig :
Or, thrown at gayer ease on some fair brow,
Let me behold, by breezy murmurs cool'd,
Broad o'er my head the verdant Cedar wave,
And high Palmetos lift their graceful shade :
Or, stretch'd amid these orchards of the sun,
Give me to drain the Cocoa's musky bowl,
And from the Palm to draw its fresh'ning wine
More bounteous far than all the frantic juice
Which Bacchus pours! Nor on its slender twigs,
Low-bending be the full Pomegranate scorn'd;
Nor, creeping thro' the woods, the gelid race,
Of Berries——oft in humble station dwells
Unboastful worth, above fastidious pomp;
Witness, thou best Anana, thou, the pride
Of vegetable life, beyond whate'er
The poets imag'd in the golden age :
Quick let me strip thee of thy tufty coat,
Spread thy ambrosial stores, and feast with Jove.

To taste the beauties of this poet's pencil,
Arabella, you must visit Bengal, where I am
more than ever convinced, he penned his
glowing descriptions of a climate and its

characteristics, Fancy, with all her fire, could
not, unassisted by facts, have suggested.
The produce of this Eastern soil is the palm,
the cocoa-nut, the tamarind, the guava, the
orange, lemon, pomegranate, pine, etc., etc.,
in the highest perfection ; nor can they be
spoken of, by an animated beholder, in terms
of common approbation. For my part, my
mental exclamation is, ''O for a muse adequate to the sublimity of the subject ! that
the wonder-working hand of Nature might be
fitly celebrated by me ! '' for, as Thomson
again expresses himself,

> Great are the scenes——————————
> ——————————that see, each circling year,
> Returning suns and double seasons pass :

and poetry, Arabella, is the natural language
where all is loveliness, and magnificence, and
power exhaustless as infinite. But I am lost,
you will perceive, in the immensity of my
subject : ''Come then,'' as my favourite bard
has it, of the Deity on a similar occasion—

> Come then, expressive silence ! muse his praise.

On so vast a scale, indeed, are all things in
this country, both human and divine, that if
any earth-born creature could be pardoned
the sin of ambition, it would be the Asiatics ;

nor can I doubt, from all I have already seen
and heard, that numbers of them are proud
enough to believe, and apply to themselves,
the poet's language :

> For me the mine a thousand treasures brings ;
> For me health gushes from a thousand springs ;
> Seas roll to waft me, suns to light me rise ;
> My footstool earth, my canopy the skies.

At least, we may fairly conclude the Moguls,
in their day of splendor, were of this haughty
faith, if we read the following description of
their encampments :

His residences (the Mogul emperor) during
the temperate season, which lasts four or
five months, are in the field ; and few
curiosities in the Eastern world were more
striking than his camp; for, besides the military men, (which amounted to above 100,000,
who carried their wives and families with
them) he was attended by most of the great
men in the empire, and followed by all
kinds of merchants and tradesmen from the
capital cities—in the whole, above a million of people ; and with this retinue he
made a tour of a thousand miles every
year, through some part of his dominions
and heard the complaints of his meanest

subjects (an astonishing trait in so lofty a character!) if they happened to be oppressed by his nabobs or viceroys.

A caravan, of ten thousand camels and oxen, constantly attended the camp, and brought provisions from every part of the country ; the commander of which was styled a prince, and vested with great power ; his office being to furnish the camp with provisions.

The camp was at least twenty miles in circumference, and formed in a circular manner ; the Mogul's tent and his women's being on an eminence in the centre, and separated from the rest by a high screen or enclosure ; next to which were the nobility, generals, and people of distinction, in another circle ; the rest succeeding in circles, according to their quality ; the inferior people being nearest the outside of the camp : nor do I marvel, that such an emperor, at such a period, should be induced, in the vanity of his heart, to style himself the Governor of the Universe, the Ornament of the Earth, etc., etc., as is the custom, on the assumption of the imperial diadem ; though, in the present circumscribed condition of the empire, those high-sounding

titles are totally inapplicable. But to descend to humbler subjects.

The East India Company, I find, pay the
rent of such houses as the captains of their
ships occupy during their residence at Calcutta ;
and it is well they do, or it would be a
heavy tax upon their purse ; for, could you
suppose it possible such a sum as 500 sacre
rupees (sixty pounds) per month, could be
decently demanded, or chearful y paid, by
these birds of passage ? it is, nevertheless, the
fact : accordingly, those gentlemen, who have
it in their power, build elegant dwelling-houses,
at the expense of 30, 40, 50, and 60,000 rupees
for the purpose of letting them ready furnished ;
and, I am assured I shall see many, which
bear the astonishing rent of 900 and 1,000
pounds sterling per year, without a table,
chair, or one necessary unhired at an equally
extravagant rate.

The streets of Calcutta, at the part of the
town inhabited by trades-people (who, by the
way, are all Blacks, except what are called
the Europe shops, of which I shall speak hereafter) are distinguished by the name of *beisars*,
or traders, by which they are occupied ; as,
the bada beisar, (fruit and pastry) ; the muchee

beisar, (the fish-market); the dewdwallar
beisar (milk-sellers); suedwallar beisar, (hog-
merchants); chine beisar, (sugar-venders),
etc., etc. Moreover curds form a separate
article of merchandise, and the shops for selling
them furnish one whole street—a proof of
their great consumption and value in the East.

The Europe shops, as you will naturally
conclude, are those ware-houses where all the
British finery imported is displayed and purchased ; and such is the spirit of many ladies
on visiting them, that there have been instances
of their spending 30 or 40,000 rupees in
one morning, for the decoration of their
persons ; on which account many husbands are
observed to turn pale as ashes, on the bare
mention of their wives being seen to enter
them : but controul is not an article of matrimonial rule at Calcutta ; and the men are
obliged to make the best of their conjugal
mortifications.

Five streets, well built, and inhabited alone
by persons of genteel rank, open on the
Esplanade, which is ornamented to a great
extent, in view of the first houses of each (one
of which is the Governor's) with iron palisades,
and makes a magnificent appearance. I

shall enlarge upon this subject as soon as I
have made my intended tour through the
town ; the whole of which, however, is a flat
situation, and the habitations are scattered
over a great space of ground ; for the gardens,
particularly the Company's and Governor's,
are extensive ; nor are the private ones
small ; for, as it is one of the chief pleasures
of the country, to admire the beauties of
vegetation, enjoy the shade, and feed on the
delicacies so bountifully bestowed by Nature,
it is their pride to possess them altogether
in their prime excellence, to speak at once
their fine taste and abundant fortune to every
beholder.

What a motley epistle is this ! the great
sublime, succeeded by the most inferior topics ;
but, Arabella, these transitions are not
to be avoided on a spot where vivacity and
dignity of mind is. transient, and a low ebb
of both the one and the other, the consequence
of languor not to be resisted, and of gusts of
heat not to be described.

I am,

Yours, as usual,

S. G.

LETTER VIII.

How prophetic were my words, Arabella, where I mention my apprehensions of the refusals I should be called upon to make !— A painful task to a feeling and not illiberal mind ; but we must all submit to our destiny.

An *old* fellow, with an incredible fortune, ogles me, and professes his life depends on his obtaining the honour of my hand—my father smiles—and I, with an air of indolent complacence (the air of the country) receive his devoirs as the just tribute of my transcendent charms ; which charms (it is already got into circulation) are held by me above all price (for the fetter of my vow has not yet transpired) ; which may possibly tend to a diminution in the train of my adorers, at least on the arrival of the next ships ; for, as the life of a butterfly is but an hour, so the ladies, who wish to see themselves advantageously disposed of, must reprobate the antediluvian practice, and be careful not to let the iron grow cold on the anvil ; which, with few exceptions, is the universal conduct : so that, I doubt not, I shall soon behold this love-stricken greybeard at the feet of some more yielding damsel :—and may she make him as happy as she will flatter herself his wealth can render her ; nor once experience the common fate of such expectations—finding she has been self-deceived.

There is also a little dapper fellow, in a yellow silk coat, that buzzes soft things in my ear, and affects to keep all the rest of his sex at a distance : but I have given it in commission to Mrs. Hartly, to hint to him that such behaviour is not lawful ; the accepted lover alone being entitled to monopolize his fair one. I suppose we shall have him in the pouts on the occasion ; this is, however, no formidable circumstance at Calcutta, where you may chuse and refuse at will.

What gives the men such constant access to the ladies their rank entitles them to visit, is, that on being once introduced, you make their abode an home—walk in and out a pleasure—have your chair and attendant ready for you, as a matter of course—and the only wonder is, what can have become of your new friends, if they happen to absent themselves without a declared engagement. At breakfast, they tell me the news of the day ; at dinner, solicit me to drink so many glasses of wine with them, that I ring unending changes

on negative phrases (and those the best chosen)
to prove my fund of polite language, and soften my cruel denials ; at the card-table they
lose their money with a good grace ; and at
supper, are brilliant companions : nor be it
unobserved by you (tho' your matrimonial
chance is beyond measure critical) you do not
forfeit your claims to homage or adoration, on
becoming a wife ; whence slander is often busy.
The opportunities are, indeed, inconceiveable
for amour, if the inclination be prompt ; but
I verily believe, that gallantry at Calcutta is,
like gallantry in France, carried on by friendly compact amongst all parties ; "I trust you
with my wife—you trust me with yours ";—
and that the abuse of such well-bred confidence
is a rare instance of the ill effects thereof.

One of two offers, for their generosity and
respectability, have been noticed by my
father ; and, with every profession of gratitude, declined by me. Mrs. Hartly remon-
strates, from looking forward (she kindly
says) to alarms such conduct gives rise to—
from implying some European engagement,
that must eventually deprive her of my company. I assure her she is mistaken, I
perceive, in vain ; for it appears to her an

absurdity, to believe, a heart, that possesses its freedom, should shut the door against unexceptionable overtures. I own, Arabella, I cannot account for it myself, unless it can be possible that the multitude renders me indifferent to individuals, and, true it is, that you have not leisure for the observations so necessary to be made previous to an union for life, in these crouded scenes; or (if you can pardon the seeming levity) sufficient time to know your own mind; one agreeable impression being immediately, if not chased away, blended with another : in short, my hour of attachment is not come ; and I never will be prevailed upon to separate, or (what is the same thing) endanger the separation of my hand and heart.

Was there any prospect of your coming to Bengal, I might, perhaps, think otherwise than, I am convinced, I ever shall do, with the reflection on events that would prevent our ever meeting more.

I am, etc.,
S. G.

LETTER IX.

I ADORE the customs of the East. Instead of having their servants, or beisars (trades-people) speaking in broken words, and mistaking, consequently misrepresenting, what their superiors say, the dresses and accommodations of the Europeans do not more perfectly discriminate them than their language ; every person taking the trouble, or rather considdering it their amusement, to learn to ask for what they want in Gentoo phrases ; and making English the vehicle only of polite conversation.

Early this morning, the weather beginning to be settled, I took advantage of a cool breeze, and was conveyed in a phaeton through the town and its environs.

THE WRITERS' BUILDINGS,

Arabella, in like manner with our Inns of Court, are divided into chambers, more or less elegant, according to the rank and consequence of their owners. This, I need not tell you, is the nursery of all the great men ; for, from being writers, they are advanced, as their abilities enable them, to the highest civil offices, or even military, if their genius inclines

them that way. I was struck by them altogether, as the monument of commercial prosperity ; and made some comments on the subject that did credit, I was told, to my sensibility and understanding ;—but I seek not to
shine in your sight, Arabella ; you know the
height and depth of my intellectual endowments, and honour me accordingly. A little
ostentation is necessary in the East ; but
English estimates run upon the softer merits ;
for we are there taught to believe, that a
woman's noblest station is retreat—for that,
as the poet says,

> Her fairest virtues fly from public sight,
> Domestic worth, that shuns too strong a light.

But, be it always remembered by you, that
Indostan is the land of vivacity, rather than
that of sentiment.

At the back of the Writers' Buildings is the

CALCUTTA THEATRE ;

the inside of which I have not yet seen ;
but am informed, from good authority,
that it equals the most splendid European
exhibition.

The performers, Arabella, are all gentlemen,
who receive no kind of compensation, but

form a fund of the admission-money, to de-
fray the expenses of the house. It consists
only of pit and boxes : to be admitted to the
first of which, you pay eight rupees (twenty
shillings)´; to the last, a gold mohr (forty
shillings) ; it is not, therefore, wonderful it
should be rendered a brilliant spectacle.

I was also shewn, *en passant*, a tavern
called the London Hotel, where entertainments
are furnished at the *moderate* price of a gold
mohr a head exclusive of the dessert and wines
—two very expensive articles indeed ! for
claret, notwithstanding its free consumption,
is in private families five rupees (twelve and
sixpence) a bottle. Of their desserts I shall
speak hereafter.

At the coffee-houses your single dish of
coffee costs you a rupee (half-a-crown) ; which
half-crown, however, franks you to the perusal
of the English newspapers, which are regular-
ly arranged on a file, as in London ; together
with the *Calcutta Advertiser*, the *Calcutta
Chronicle*, etc., etc.—and, for the honour of
Calcutta, be it recorded, that the two last-
named publications *are*, what the English
prints formerly *were*, moral, amusing, and
intelligent. I wish, Arabella, you could turn

this hint to profit ; but much fear the frenzy
of politics and the fever of scandal are confirmed diseases, and, as such, incurable.

Nor is Calcutta unfurnished with Livery
Stables, riding being much the fashion at certain seasons of the year. And I had a distant
view of the Hospital, a building that deviates
from the general plan of architecture, being
three stories high ; and I am told, it deserves
my particular notice and inspection.

At the Old Fort, which is situated at the
extremity of those streets terminated by the
Esplanade (I shudder to name it) are the ruins
of the Black Hole, where the no less memorable
than tragical event took place in 1756 ; for,
out of one hundred and forty-five British subjects, only twenty-three survived the horrors
of one night's imprisonment : amongst those
saved, was Mr. Holwell, the Governor's chief
servant, who has written a most affecting account thereof. The cause of this melancholy
catastrophe was a quarrel of the Nabob, or
Mogul Viceroy, Surajah Dowla, with the Company—who suddenly invested Calcutta with a
large body of black troops ; the then Governor
and some of the other principal persons threw
themselves and their chief effects on board

the ships in the river; whilst they who remained, for some hours bravely defended the place; but, their ammunition being expended, were compelled to surrender on tolerably flattering terms.

The Soubah, a capricious and unfeeling tyrant, instead, however, of observing the capitulation, forced his prisoners into a secure hold, only about eighteen feet square, and shut them in from almost all communication of free air. But, I draw a shade over miseries I am unequal to paint; and will only add, that the seasonable arrival of our countrymen, Lord Clive and Admiral Watson, put the English once more (with some difficulty) in possession of Calcutta; the insensible Nabob, after plundering the place, having returned to his capital, under the persuasion that he had totally routed and subdued them; and the war was concluded by the battle of Plassey, as you may read in the British annals, won by Colonel Clive, and the death of Surajah Dowla; in whose stead Mhir Jaffier, one of his generals, a friend to the English, was advanced to the Nabobship; and Calcutta flourished more than ever, and became what we find it at this day

The Old Fort is now totally deserted, and, except the church, has few buildings to boast ; nor is its custom otherwise occupied than by the landing of copper, etc., etc., for the Company's service.

The recollection of what I have related, so affected my spirits, that I begged to return home ; and, having committed my morning's excursion to paper, shall endeavour to remember the concluding part of it no more.

One very singular circumstance at Calcutta is, Arabella, that there are no nurseries in any of the houses ; nor does a child (with few exceptions) make its appearance.

Having made the observation upon repeated occasions (for you know I delight much in the company of children) I could not forbear asking Mrs. Hartly, how it came to pass that no little folks had met my eyes ? She, smiling, replied (for she is a sweet, amiable woman) "suspend your curiosity until to morrow, and this mystery shall be unravelled." Accordingly, at the usual early time the ensuing morn, we set off in our palanquins on a journey, the motive of which I was not aware of ; and soon arrived at a most romantic and beautiful spot, at about five

miles distance from our place of residence ;
where it was revealed to me, the infant part
of the family (as is the custom of the country)
was situated ; and I had the pleasure of making an instantaneous acquaintance with a
boy and girl, lovely as cherubs, and innocent
as lovely.

These retreats (which in England we should
know by the name of villas) are at Calcutta
called *Bungilos,* and possess all the charms
and beauties of rural existence. The description of one of them, however, will serve for
all, with only the necessary and natural abate-
ments, fortune, taste, and liberality, produce
in every instance.

Hartly Bungilo consists of a suite of apartments on a ground floor, with a thatched roof
and verandas, and stands in the centre of a
garden, I am wholly at a loss to describe to
you. Imagine, therefore, to yourself a spot,
adorned with all the choicest flowers with
which you are acquainted, formed into
espaliers, and encircling the fairest parterre
your eyes ever beheld ; with recesses, such
as queen Dido would have admired, and
temples the Graces might not disdain to
visit ; with, moreover, a spacious tank or

fish-pond at certain distances—every footstep
appearing fairy ground, and every breeze
perfume.

My surprise and pleasure diverted Mrs.
Hartly exceedingly. " Take my advice another time," said she ; " and, instead of enquiring into things you are unacquainted with,
endeavour to behold them, and judge for
yourself." " Had I told you, in so many
words, that my little boy and girl were, with
whatever suitable attendance, living in a
thatched house, whilst I occupied what you
called a palace—would you not have shook
your head, and .changed your opinion of a
woman you now profess to esteem ? Whereas, beholding them lodged in the bosom of
free air and tranquility, jessamine and roses
forming their bed, and peace and joy their
pillow—will you not own, that mothers at
Calcutta have their children's happy condition
as much at heart, as in a country, where at the
top of the house, they are trusted to the care
of mere hirelings, and much farther removed
from the maternal superintendence than in
our bungilos ; though those bungilos are
under the regulation of well-educated and
well-principled gentlewomen, whose time and

talents are devoted, in return for a handsome
stipend, to their service and benefit."

I had no reply ready ; therefore only pressed
her hand, in silent approbation : but she
is discernment at all points, and every movement is to her intelligence.

Tell me, my dear girl, if you can, why the
genuine delight of conversing with children
is so seldom sought for ? To me, next to
angels, I love and revere them. The dawnings
of their reason are considered by me as so
many emanations of the Divinity, and their
artless turns of fancy the most rational of
human entertainments.

My little new friends had not been five
minutes presented to me before they found
out the weak side of my character ; and, having
won me, to all intents and purposes, to their
wishes, engaged me by a solemn promise (which
I will actually perform) to visit them every
morning I can contrive to steal from the company of Hartly House. But most transient
are our pleasurable moments in this world :
I was summoned to re-ascend my palanquin
at the end of two hours, (the fleetest of all the
hours I had spent at Calcutta) and was brought
home with the actual loss of my heart—an

acknowledgment that gave rise to innumerable effusions of Eastern gallantry, wholly
unacceptable to me, and, as such, wholly dis-
regarded.

It is usual, it seems, at a certain age, to send
the sons and daughters of this golden world
to England for education ; but great improve-
ments having been made during this last
quarter of a century in every branch of polite
and valuable knowledge, among the Calcut-
tonians, this, together with the terrors of the
ocean, which await such infant fugitives, has
induced many fond fathers and mothers, as
well as Mr. and Mrs. Hartly, to make it worth
an accomplished Englishwoman's while to
form their manners, etc., etc., under the parental auspices. The *gouvernante* at Hartly
Bungilo, who comes precisely under this description, is the widow of a clergyman—has a
pleasing person, and a well-stored mind—and
was prevailed upon to make the voyage on the
consideration of 250 gold mohrs (500 pounds)
to be paid to her on her arrival; where she lives
with as much discretion as elegance, and is
esteemed and honoured by all who know her.

A large *bouquet* (every flower of which, by
appearing more beautiful than the last noticed,

I had selected from the multitude) was ordered to be carried for me to Calcutta. Nature
is here lavish of her most beautiful productions ;
and so peculiarly attentive to gratify the eye
and the scent, that it is impossible to bring the
island of your existence into the smallest com-
petition with the air I now breathe, or the objects I behold—a great denial, you will perceive, to the unceasing remembrance of you,
I have so repeatedly assured you of ; as a
healer for which breach of faith and truth, I
have hit upon a proposal, that, if you are
human, must have attraction for you. The
Nabob, Arabella, a young smart fellow, lives
but at the distance of four miles from Hartly
House. He has, it is true, several wives already ; but you shall be his wife of wives ; and
as for his copper complexion, you are too
wise to make that an objection. Come then,
and dwell only a short time with us—let him
behold your face, and have a few opportunities of discovering the perfections of your
temper, and he will think no price too high
to purchase your friendship and affection. I
should rejoice to see you a Nabobess, that
you may surpass me as much in rank, as you
surpass me in every personal and mental

accomplishment. But you are so sentimental,
there is no dealing with you ; and I expect, in
the lines of your beloved Young, I shall be
asked, by way of answer to my wild question,

Can wealth give happiness ?—look round and see
What gay distress, what splendid misery!

which is so truly English, there is no standing ;
I therefore hasten to conclude myself.

Yours etc., etc.

S. G.

LETTER X.

THE manners of the ladies at Calcutta are
somewhat contradictory—now all softness and
femininity, and now all courage and resolution ;
as you shall hear :

They take a particular pleasure, on the one
hand, in obliging and informing strangers—
melt into tears at every tale of sorrow—and
sweetly sympathize with those whose spirits
are depressed ; on the other hand, you behold
them so little attentive to female decorum
and so fearless of danger, that a scarlet
riding dress, which gives them most the appearance of the other sex, enraptures them—

and, to drive a phaeton and pair with a vivacity, a *dégagement*, or whatever may be the
proper epithet, to mark their skill and uncon-
cern, in the midst of numberless spectators, is
their delight ; whilst I, on beholding every such
exhibition, say, with Dr. Young,

——Such charioteers as these
May drive six harness'd monarchs if they please ;

for, to characterize them completely in your
sight, I must add, that the ladies of gaiety
and *ton* always make a point on these occasions, of having a gentleman companion, who
lolls at his ease ; the office of managing the
reins, etc., etc., being wholly assumed by the
lady. I wish, nevertheless, you could see
these phaeton enterprises ; for their attendance
and accompaniments are in the high style of
Eastern etiquette. A servant, in the dress
I have heretofore repeatedly described, runs
on each side of the horses, with long-handled
flappers in their hands, sometimes holding by
their manes, and sometimes at a little distance ;
and the effect is both striking and pleasing. The phaetons are English built, and
ornamented with all the taste that country can
boast, and all the expence the Asiatics are forward to incur, for their exterior importance ;

—the horses finely and splendidly set out,
with silver nets to guard their necks from
insects, and reins elegantly decorated :—and,
to finish the whole, a kittesaw is suspended,
nor unfrequently, over the lady's head—
which gives her the true Eastern grandeur
of appearance.

Lady C—m—rs, who, by the way, is
one of the examples of the unions which here
take place, (I mean as to the disparity of age)
is one of the most celebrated on this fashionable list ; and, for attendant beaux, both as to
smartness and variety, yields to no one.

Mrs. Hartly is, however, of quite another
order of beings, and, like myself is the daughter of an East India captain, but conveyed
by her father to Calcutta much earlier in life ;
she— has, therefore, or at least I imagine so,
imbibed all their amiable prejudices, and
thinks matrimony the duty of every young
woman who meets with an offer she cannot
disapprove ;—for she persuades herself, and
perhaps, on experience, that esteem is the
best basis of affection, and best security for
our rejoicing in the choice we make ; for what
is love (a propensity to approve, without the
sanction of reason or the pause of sentiment)

she affirms, blinds the understanding, and
causes us to rest satisfied with pleasing manners, with too little attention to moral
rectitude ; an error in judgment, and a self-
desertion, she asserts, we smart under to
the latest moment of our existence. I
am, nevertheless, unconvinced and uncon-
verted.

She is, however, perfectly free from those
traits of affectation which are so generally
conspicuous in a flattered woman (and flattery at Calcutta is, literally speaking, our
daily bread) has a cultivated understanding
and a feeling of heart, and is at once the
honour and happiness of her husband ; my
beloved mother, moreover, expired in her
friendly arms : judge then, if she is not dear
to me ! But these are the very things that
constitute my danger ; for I know, though
she knows it not, that without a congenia-
lity of taste, of sentiment, of vivacity, and
of seriousness there is no chance of felicity for
me as a wife. In a word, Arabella, my father
is the model of him I can ever love, or ever
wish to unite my destiny with ; and, until I
meet with this *rara avis* (for well you know
the treasures of his head, the treasures of his

heart and most agreeable person) I am **determined** to remain.

S. G.

LETTER XI.

I AM half frantic with delight!—A review, Arabella!—What English *female* heart vibrates not at the bare mention of a review? We are to dine in the New Fort, at the commanding officer's (the ·Fort Major) whose house is situated within its circumference; and it is deemed one of the finest forts in the world, has a chain across the river, to secure the harbour from invasion, covers near five miles of ground, and has the bustling charms of a garrison.

This fort, which was created by the East India Company, at an immense expense, is, I find, the nursery for forming and disciplining the troops from England; and it is with pleasure I am enabled to assure you, that they are provided for in an ample manner, when in garrison, and kindly treated; which, in fact, is very different to the notions entertained,

and the opinions circulated, in England —
It is true that, when called forth into the
field, their duty is not easily performed, the
intense heat of the climate being hard to support; but, in order to throw in every possible
softening, their pay is augmented to twelve
rupees (forty shillings) a month, which aug-
mentation is called *Batta-money*—and as a
proof of the advantages held out to them, one
of these common soldiers, who was shewn to
me a few days before he embarked, left India
with seven hundreds pounds of his own ac-
quiring, for England! Yet it is doubtful
whether he will remain there or not ; for few revisit their native country who do not, after a
short period, re-enter the East India service.

The barracks, I am informed, are very fine,
of course the men are comfortably lodged ;
and, as it is the interest, so it is obviously the
desire of the Company, to keep them neat in
their lodging, their persons, and their feeding,
(death and dirt being synonymous in this
climate) the last is therefore diligently guarded against to prevent the dire ravages of the
first.

The garrison consists, you must understand,
almost solely of the Company's troops, the

Government forces being seldom quartered there. These soldiery are, however, held in high respect, and form a regular guard of centinels at the Governor's and the other great officers' houses and also patrole the streets, as members of the police, to clear them of such nuisances as they would otherwise be liable to, and particularly from sailors when in a state of inebriety : and over this part of the military a Town Major presides, who belongs to the Company, and is the regulating officer, or general intendant, on all occasions.

Near the Fort is the hospital I have already mentioned, erected for the reception of *all* indisposed persons, from whatever cause ; throughout which, the wards or chambers are so neat and accommodating, that wretchedness reposes, and malady is put to flight.— It is lighted and cooled by verandas, and every possible means are adopted to procure the free circulation of air, etc., etc., and it is allowed, by all who have seen it, to be superior to every thing under that appellation in the universe : nor could I forbear on viewing it, exclaiming,

These are Imperial works, and worthy kings.

I was, however, informed immediately, by one present, of the source and nature of its establishment ; and find it was built by the united contributions of the Europeans of Calcutta and the Company.—Yes, Arabella, this blessed asylum originates from commerce and owes its support solely to commerce ; —and observe, so charmed am I with the benevolence and the liberality of its institution, that, should I ever have an unwieldy fortune to leave behind me, the only hospital I will endow with it shall be the Hospital of Calcutta.—But I am unable to impress you with the pleasurable sensations I enjoyed, on being an eye-witness of this invaluable place of refuge and accommodation for my diseased fellow creatures and fellow-countrymen.

To gain admission into the hospital of Calcutta, there is no other interest or recommendation necessary, than being an European, and deprived of health. Morever, men of honour and humanity, tender of the lives of those received under their care, and tenacious of the just application of their subscription-money, are its visitants and superintendents ; no experiments can therefore be tried, at the hazard of a worthy, though humble individual's

safety ; no harpy keepers can grind the face
of the patients, or riot in plenty, whilst they
are expiring from wretchedness and neglect ;
nor is a single nurse continued, that fails to
perform the duties of her engagement : and
the manifold restored patients prove the utility and the benevolence of the institution.

I blush, Arabella, to feel, that all I have
written, as I have it from my father's assertion, is an impeachment of the customs (in
this instance) in my native country ; and it
would be god-like in you to promote new and
salutary regulations, by publishing so noble
an example as I have thus set before you

I am so struck with these matters, that I
cannot forbear making them the frequent subjects of my conversation ; extolling the country I now reside in ; and sighing for the disgraces of the country I have quitted ; and,
could you but behold the fixed attention of my
auditors, you would smile—but, in the pastoral language of Shenstone,

> They love me the more when they hear
> Such tenderness fall from my tongue.

I was prevailed upon to be mistress of a
phaeton in this excursion ; but so *outré* should
I have exhibited myself, that I intreated my

father would let me drive him. This was not granted. An exchange was, however, settled that was equally to my satisfaction ; for Mrs. Hartly took my father with her and I had her husband for my cicisbeo. O Arabella ! if you knew half Mr. Hartly's virtues—filial, conjugal, paternal, universal—you would rise up and say, this is a man worthy—worthy female respect, worthy masculine celebrity ; yet does he appear perfectly unconscious of his own merit, and is the first to praise, and the last to condemn, every person living that is mentioned before him. I think I must devote one entire letter to his history, notwithstanding subject matter flows in upon me so rapidly, that I am at a loss what to give the preference to. I am, indeed, aware, that the colour of my own mind is apt to bias my choice ; and that I rather entertain you with what interests my feelings, or flatters my fancy, than such particulars as may be best entitled to your perusal ;—it is an error I will endeavour to correct, when I next give myself an opportunity of assuring you, that I am,

Your's, etc.,

S. G.

LETTER XII.

THE party to-day was brilliant——all that
pomp and splendor could do, was done, to
conceal the ravages of burning suns ; and
never were military gentlemen more animated,
more obsequious, or camp more delightful ;
but Mars in the East, like Hercules at the
court of Omphale has more gallantry than
hostility about him.

Between Chitpore, the Nabob's house, and
the Fort, at a place called Bugee Bugee, a
perpetual encampment, *in terrorem,* I imagine, is kept up, to prevent any fatal surprise
for the future ; and a very pretty appearance
it makes ; but you will, no doubt, as it is situated in the very neighbourhood, hear more
of it in future ; for the review, of which I have
been so happy a spectator, is quite a distinct
and separate entertainment.

The troops performed all their evolutions
with equal credit to themselves and their
commanders : nevertheless, from my acquaintance with the gentlemen, etc , etc., the whole
display had, to me, more of a public shew,
cal ulated to please the ladies, than to alarm
the enemies of the Company by their skilful
manœuvrings ; for which gay and giddy idea I

beg the gentlemen's pardon—and very candidly acknowledge, that though their great complaisance has removed every idea of terror from my mind, yet the utility of these reviews may be very great; for (besides keeping the soldiers in practice) the minds they are intended to influence behold them in a quite different light, and tremble at the idea of their prowess.

We had a superb gala at the Fort Major's; who is so agreeable a man, Arabella, that I detected myself in the act of enquiring, whether he was married or single. His lady, however, very opportunely appeared, to save my credit, and reconcile me to myself; for she evidently merited and engaged my entire approbation, without any alloy.

She made me many pretty compliments; and, whilst I beheld her, and listened to her, I became impatient to know whether she had a little family or not (for it is my wish to be acquainted with all the children at Calcutta), and I have obtained her promise to introduce me at her Bungilo in a short time.

I am told, this passion for the society of children is the characteristic of an unvitiated taste : it may be so ; but of this I am certain that the politeness of the people of Calcutta

is such, that what is not vice, they will exalt
into virtue ; and what is, they will melt down,
by their charitable report, into error and misfortune.

You can have no notion of the *nonchalance*
and dégagement with which I conducted
myself through the day ; but you will recollect
that women who are accustomed to live with
a multitude of men, acquire a *modest* assurance
(let me call it) private education cannot bestow.
—Friendship and respect are the sentiments
reciprocally professed, and chearfulness and
joy the universal objects : therefore, those who
can do the kindest, or say the pleasantest
things, are unquestionably the most esteemed
companions ; for Othello's liberal-mindedness
seems to prevail throughout (at least) all my
agreeable connections.

> " 'Tis not to make me jealous, to say my wife
> is fair, loves company, sings, dances well,
> &c. &c. ; for, where virtue is, these are most
> virtuous."

I am sensible I am not correct in my quotation ; but a visit to your library will enable
you to read it at large, for both your instruct-
tion and amusement.

But, instead of ending this letter *en militaire*
as was my intention, I must touch upon a
circumstance that I advert to with a sigh.—
In my (*dear*, I had almost called it) native
country, existence is pleasing far beyond the
period at which it becomes painful here ; the
early maturity of the natives leading down to
early decay ; insomuch, that you would be
shocked to behold a woman of thirty ; for her
appearance, Arabella, is equal, in infirmity
and wrinkles, at least, to the oldest looking
woman in England at three score. Both sexes
marry young, have families, decline, depart,
and are remembered only in their offspring.
—Not so the Europeans, even at Calcutta—
having received their birth in the happy zone
of your residence, Arabella, their nerves are
much stronger strung ; their youth, moreover,
is passed under the same healthful meridian ;
which enables them to endure the Eastern
sun for ten or twelve years of their mid-
life with tolerable satisfaction ; and their days
are lengthened into old age by their return
to Britain. But we will quit this melancholy
side of the prospect if possible, forever.

The Nabob, I need not tell you, is merely
a Viceroy to the Mogul, in like manner with

your Lord Lieutenant of Ireland, and the re-
presentative of his most sublime master.   Formerly his residence was at a distance from Calcutta, and his intercourse with the Europeans
restricted to embassies ; but now his palace of
Chitpore (for well does it deserve the name of
a palace) is only four miles, as I have already
told you, from Hartly House ; and on such
friendly terms does he live with the military
gentlemen that he gives them entertainments of
dinners, fire-works, etc., etc. at an immense expence ; but always eats alone, according to the
customs of the Asiatic Mahometans, seated on
the ground, which is over-spead by superb
carpets (by the way, the only carpets I have
heard of in India—the fine matting being, for
coolness, substituted in their place) ; and, what
will surprise you is, that the captain or commanding officer of the Nabob's guards, which
consist of a whole battalion of black troops, is
an Englishman, a younger brother of an ennob-
led family, and who paid £80,000 (acquired in
this world of wealth) for the appointment.

The uniform of this battalion is the same
worn by the Company's troops—red turned
up with white,—with turbans to distinguish
the divisions thereof.

The exterior of Chitpore in some degree
bespeaks the grandeur of its owner ; but I am
informed few things exceed the magnificence
of its interior architecture and ornaments.
The apartments are immense—the baths
elegant—and the seraglio, though a private one,
suitable, in every particular, to the rest of the
building : nor must the gardens be unmen-
tioned ; for they not only cover a wide extent of
ground, but are furnished with all the beauties
and perfumes of the vegetable kingdom.
When he rides out, a detachment of his black
troops attend him ;—and observe, Arabella, the
Nabob's *salam* (the word for compliment from
his soldiers) is a most graceful application of
the back part of the hand to the front of the
turban, with a slight bend of the head.

But I should tell you, all persons of any
rank have in addition to the servants I have
described a *salam-bearer* ; and the note or card,
containing compliments of whatever kind
is called a *chit* :—nor is there a morning that
my toilet is not covered with *salams* and *chits*,
to the no small gratification of my pride, and
support of my consequence.

Billiards are much played at Calcutta—a
game well adapted, in my opinion, to the con-

venience of the country—it requiring no great
exertions of either body or mind : but I retract that opinion on the instant ; for the sums
won and lost must keep the blood in a perpetual fever, even to endangering the life of the
parties. In private families, the billiard is
a kind of state-room. At the coffee-houses,
you are accommodated with tables and attendants for eight *anas*, or half rupees, by candle-
light, or six by day-light, a certain number
of hours—every coffee-house having at least
two tables ; so that men of spirit have as many
fashionable opportunites of ruining themselves
here as you Europeans can boast. I lament
this abuse of understanding ; but fashionable
vices are the hardest of all others to eradicate ;
and, that it will ever become fashionable to
be moral or well-judging, I have my doubts
and apprehensons. You, my dear girl, are a
blessed exception. I have friends around me,
at this moment, that are your counterpart,
and models of all that is good or great in
the human character.—I have written myself
into the spleen, and will therefore bid you
good night.

I HAVE told you, here are livery-stables. I now add, that horses are cheap at Calcutta; and, what you would little expect to hear of, racers are bred for the turf.

The race-ground is a distinct part of the Esplanade; and the horses that run for a subscription-plate, as in England, are fed, they inform me, with meal, as you English feed pigeons; and I shall soon have it in my power to give you 'a complete description of this amusement in the East, as the annual period is now not far distant.

I have resumed my pen; for Mr. Hartly and my father are not, I find, yet returned from spending the evening at the governor's; —and though though palanquins are safe conveyances and their company numerous, I must hear they are come home before I attempt to repose for the night, or more properly, morning; for it is now more than half after three.

Palanquins are, indeed, such state appendages, that, if a gentleman at Calcutta (which is frequently the case) chuses to walk when on a visiting party, his palanquin must follow him in the same form, in every particular, as if he himself was within; a departure

therefrom being deemed a solecism in
polite etiquette.

Bless me! what do I hear? Drums and
musical instruments—and the streets are
suddenly illuminated. What can it mean?—
Mrs. Hartly is, however, at my door; and I
may, perhaps, have it in my power, before
I conclude, to make amends for this very
dull epistle.

A Gentoo marriage procession, Arabella,
and an extreme pretty one too, was the novelty my ever-attentive friend to my amusement, Mrs. Hartly, called upon me to be a
spectator of.

The bride was carried in an elegant palanquin (did I ever tell you the difference between a lady's and a gentleman's palanquin?
I believe not) with tassels of immense finery
(the distinguishing decoration for ladies) and
near forty couple of men preceding, and
an equal number following it; with wreaths
of flowers beautifully fancied, and lights without number. After which came the bridegroom in his palanquin also, with great ceremony, and as many attendants as his bride;
but not one woman, except herself, in the
whole procession.

The musicians played the most lively tunes imaginable, and the company danced in pairs as they passed along, making use of the wreath, with nearly as much taste and good effect as the figure dancers in your London theatres ; and in this manner they proceed, it seems, through the whole town——the Gentoos, and their Padras (the Bramins) living all around it.

They live, Arabella, (except from the austerities, in some instances, in their religion) the most inoffensively and happily of all created beings——their Pythagorean tenets teaching them, from their earliest infancy, the lesson of kindness and benevolence ; nor do they intentionally hurt any living thing :—— from their temperance they derive health, and from the regulation of their passions, contentment ; and come immediately under that description of Pope :

> They ask no angel's wings, no seraph's fire ;
> But think, admitted to their native sky,
> Their faithful dog shall bear them company.

I shall, however, make it my business, now my curiosity is awakened and interested, to learn all possible intelligence of a people so peculiar, and so distinct from the rest of the world——and one door of knowledge can be easily opened upon me; for the Sekars are all Gentoos (a kind of brokers) under whose care the East India captains put their merchandize, and who fix the rates of purchase according to the ebbs and flows of the supplies intrusted to their superintendence ; and many of them amass large fortunes. Their profits are established, and their faith unimpeached ; and they are found so necessary, that it is impossible to dispose of European goods without their assistance or notice : moreover, any of the Company's servants who arrive in the India ships and bring property with them, on application to a Sekar are furnished with whatever money they stand in need of, without bond or other legal security ; for a breach of moral rectitude on the part of the borrower would be productive of indelible disgrace and personal danger—the Company protecting these Gentoo brokers, notaries, or factors, in their lawful rights.

My father, you know, is that sort of man who steals the love of all who know him; accordingly, his Sekar, though a Gentoo, and though such intercourse is unusual, has

attached himself to his employer by the heartfelt ties of friendship and affection—walks in
and out of Hartly House at pleasure—and
converses by signs with me, with many marks
of high approbation. He has, moreover, I
find, a relation that is a young Bramin ; and
(shall I own to you a most extravagant piece of
vanity which has recently sprung up in my
mind?) an admirer, Arabella, of his character
would be to me a proof of my attarctions I
should be proud of.

I will tell Mrs. Hartly my whim, and engage
his relation to introduce him. The compliments I at present receive, are all of the
commonplace kind, and may with equal
propriety be addressed to any sister female ;
but to please a Bramin I must have perfections of the mental sort, little inferior
to the purity and the benignity of angels :—
in a word, my good dispositions would be
cultivated and brought forward by such an
acquaintance, and my bad ones corrected ;
and, as celibacy is their engagement, the
soul would be the only object of attachment
and admiration.

You will, I suppose, conclude flattery has
turned my head ; but, to be serious, it would

delight my peculiar taste to converse with
beings of so superior an order, and to become
an humble copy of their exemplary and beautiful simplicity.

What a transition !—but it is not my fault;
for my father, on coming home, told me, as an
agreeable piece of news, that the theatre will
open next week—and I rejoiced beyond measure to hear it.

Though, you must understand the stage of
Calcutta is under regulations which Britain
has renounced ; for there are no female performers ;——and I could most heartily wish
that this reproach of morality could be done
away in England. The custom, you know,
is foreign, and alone imported by the polished
Charles, on his return from exile in foreign
lands ; and you will not attempt, I am persuaded, to deny that this fatal change in theatrical politics has rendered the playhouses
so many nurseries of vice, or public seraglios
far more censurable and licentious than any
the Eastern world contains ;—for the difficulty here is for any male individual (except
their owner) to get into them ; whereas, in
your metropolis, every nocturnal exhibition,
of even the most sentimental drama, is an

advertisement where gentlemen, on certain
conditions, may be accommodated with a temporary companion——and I blush to recollect
the incompatibility thereof with delicacy and
propriety. But I will tell you more of my
mind on this subject, when I have seen with
what effect dress can bring forth (as ladies)
the smart young fellows of Calcutta, on theatrical ground.

What a mistake did I fall into, when I imagined that one day spent in domestic luxury
would be a picture of all the succeeding ones
I should pass!

Amusement is varied with every varying
season of the year, except the months when
the *hot winds* (what a paradox! yet it is a
reality) annoy this coast, and the rude hand
of sickness interrupts every scheme of pleasure; insomuch that, to guard your own
life at every avenue, and fortify your mind
against the wounds it must sustain in the
persons of your dying friends, is the whole
employment.

Heaven! how equal is thy bounty, and thy
goodness to the children of men!—The scenes
I now participate would be too highly fraught
with felicity, untempered by the ravages of

disease, and the distresses of heat ; for, at the seasons I have mentioned,

> ———— in blazing height of noon,
> The sun, oppress'd, is plung'd in thickest gloom :
> Still horror reigns, a dreary twilight round
> Of struggling night and day, malignant mix'd ;
> For, to the hot equator crowding fast,
> Where, highly rarefied, the yielding air
> Admits their steam, incessant vapours roll.

Whereas, in your soft climate, Arabella, such are your humble tables and humble pleasures, that all the transports of animation and of magnificence are unknown to you, and you creep through one dull track from infancy to age.

Adieu ! adieu !—There is an oriental effusion for you ! begun, I perceive, with too much solemnity for the turn I have given it ;—but I must either be painfully serious, or idly gay, when I remember the days that are gone—— days spent in the most rational delights—and in company with my (to me) lost Arabella.

Yours, etc.,

S. G.

LETTER XIII.

ON the race-ground, Arabella, (at a distance from the immediate track of the courses, you will conceive) are two trees situated, whose spreading branches afford the most delightful shade, and under which I had it in contemplation to have voted for the erection of a temple.

But behold ! on mentioning them in terms of admiration I was to my surprize told they were called the Trees of Destruction —and with great propriety, you will allow, when I add that all the duels (which are not few in this country) are fought under them.

Duels at Calcutta ?—my nature revolts at the idea !—Is not the angel of Death, then, sufficiently industrious in reducing the human race, that the arm of a friend should be uplifted against friend (which I understand is the case) on as trival provocation as in England, where the bills of mortality are so thinly filled ?

But, Arabella, (for I will be gay, in my own defence, on even the gravest subjects) is it not a most mortifying abatement of my consequence, that these charms of mine have not

yet sent two despairing, two passionate, or two
any species of contending lovers and rivals, to
die by the hands of each other, under these
same trees in my name ?

Nay, so far am I from having occasioned
a single duel, that I never suspected this con-
vivial people of the bare idea of such a thing.
—I must set to work, and, if possible, get at
the knowledge of so extraordinary a circumstance ; for I should suppose with Addison,
(from all I have seen of their gallantry and
their admiration) that, if they must quarrel,
they would think nothing worth quarrelling
about, except a fine woman,——and should
it prove (as that nevertheless favourite writer
of mine affirms) "that there is no quarrel
without a woman in it," I shall be ashamed
of my own insignificance, and break with all
my male acquaintance for their light estima-
tion of me.

If duelling is, as I am assured, the fashionable propensity, I shudder to think what dire
ills a young and beautiful coquet might cause
in this land ! But, for the peace of society,
coquetry is practised at Calcutta in a new style;
for the handsome young women (except myself, Arabella) are all wives ; and fheir adorers,

you will perceive, could not, with any decent pretext, cut each other's throats ; and few husbands are disturbed at the innocent freedoms of either manner or conversation in their *cara sposas.*

You shall not, however, with that face of your's, come among us, until I am disposed of ; for, though I am harmless where I have no competitor, having cast the eye of desire upon Chitpore, you would find me a formidable rival ;—nor do I doubt (though tilting with the Nabob would be out of the question) but I could raise a little army to oppose and combat such Europeans, at all points, as were capable of advancing your honour and glory at my expence.—And thus have I outlived the liberality of which my former letters brought you so striking a proof : but Chitpore was then unknown to me, and the Nabob, in appearance, out of my reach ; whereas now I can throw out a lure whenever I please—and who can tell what dignities are destined for,

Your's etc.,
S. G.

LETTER XIV.

I AM this evening, Arabella, invited to a
concert at the Governor's, of gentlemen performers, who, I am told, are masters of the
several instruments they undertake to exercise ; for it is the common received opinion
at Calcutta, in direct opposition to the Chesterfield tenet, that Nero himself, if he had not
sunk the emperor in the fidler, would have
done honour to the imperial diadem by
his musical taste and skill. But it was the
pride of his nature alone that was gratified
by his performances—his senses were un-
touched—his soul unharmonized—and en-
mity and death occupied his thoughts, even
in the moment his fingers called forth sounds
of delight : whereas, on the contrary, King
David, who, as we have it on sacred record,
not only played upon, but tuned his voice to
his harp, was as great a king and, with one
only exception, as good a king, as any succeeding period can boast; neither his personal dignity, or his regal reputation, being lessened
thereby.

I am going to make a distinction, which I
expect you to subscribe to ; and that is, the

distinction between dressing to the best advantage, in order to do credit to our friends, and doing so for the purpose of gratifying our vanity. Mrs. Hartly is so proud of her guests, that she proclaims their imagery, as well as real merits, far and wide : and I am sensible, in consequence of such partial reports, I am expected to be found the standard of fashion and good taste in the article of appearance.

Would it not therefore be to mortify her, and disgrace my father, if I was to fail in all possible and proper attention to my toilet ?

I have not to this day failed, I assure you ; nor is the occasion a common one. The Governor is entitled to our respect, in honour of the British sovereign, in like manner as (on a court day) the British sovereign and his amiable consort are entitled to the *salams* and superb decorations of those who present themselves at St James's.—And so much by way of apology for my splendid trappings ; for, my dear girl, I have it yet to tell you, that a set of diamond pins from the very mines of Golconda have been given me by my father, and a pair of bracelets of pearl, with gold clasps, studded with small brilliants, by Mrs. Hartly, who declares to me, that whatever I behold of her prosperity originates from the friendly support of my father I have also a necklace of pearl of more value than I chuse to mention ; and my hair will be decorated, my arms, and every part of my visible person, beyond all I can give you an idea of.

But, surprising to relate, Arabella—such are the corrected and confirmed principles of the Gentoos, that, though the diamond merchants travel with all their tempting treasures under their sole convoy without fire-arms, etc., etc., not one of them has ever been deprived of an atom of his property by this whole people. What then are we Europeans made of ? or how must we appear in their gentle and upright eyes, who have waded through the blood of millions, to bring home gems of inconsiderable value, in comparison to what these travelling merchants are possessed of ? On such recollection, I am ashamed to know myself a European : nor can it be doubted.

If there are as some tenets imply, a distinction of heavenly situations, will not this goodminded people occupy the first in rank ; for nearest to the divine attributes of any thing you can have a conception of, is their kindheartedness and probity.

I have had a harp presented to me, and am already complimented upon the delicacy of my finger. It is, you know, an instrument well adapted to this Arcadian climate ; and I have played upon it at Hartly Bungilo by moonlight.—Can I go higher in my description thereof ?

The ambition, Arabella, is, who shall have the honour of adorning the top with a wreath, the daily offering of my host of adorers ;— and I wish you could behold the well-dissembled dejection, and the well-dissembled delight, which mark the features of the rejected and approved votary : in a word, it requires very peculiar gifts to believe one's self a mortal.

Apropos of mortality—I have visited the burying-grounds, which are to me scenes of melancholy entertainment, from the affectionate fancy displayed in commemorating a departed friend ;

For many a holy text around is strewed ;

and the air of neatness, that proof of un-abating attention, which every where meets the eye, so unlike the crusts of dust which disgrace the labours of the sculptor in that first

of royal sepulchres, Westminster Abbey, and
the astonishing insensibility of the French in
this article (for in France, if we except the
monuments of their kings, not a stone tells
where they lie)—the fairest, the bravest, and the
best, are alike unnoticed and unremembered.
—Strange and unaccountable circumstance !

You have visited St. Pancras, in the neighbourhood of London ; nay, I recollect we have
visited it together, and together interchanged
our sensation on the occasion ; for there, as
we read it from the hand of the graver, are
deposited the sacred and beloved remains of
infancy, of youth, of maturity, and of age.
Alas ! Arabella, the Bengal burying grounds
(for there are two of them) though they greatly
resemble that   churchyard in monumental
erections, bear a melancholy testimony to the
truth of my observations on the short date
of existence in this climate.

Born just to bloom and fade,

is the chief intelligence you receive from the
abundant memorials of dissolved attachments
and lamented relatives.

Obelisks, pagodas, etc., are erected at great
expence ; and the whole spot is surrounded

by as well-turned a walk as those you tra-
verse in Kensington Gardens, ornamented with
a double row of aromatic trees, which afford
a solemn and beautiful shade : in a word, not
old Windsor churchyard, with all its cypress
and yews, is in the smallest degree compara-
ble to them'; and I quitted them with unspeak-
able reluctance.

There is no difference between these two
grounds, but in the expence of the monuments,
which denote that persons of large fortune
are there interred, and *vice versa* ; whence, in
order to preserve this difference in the appearance, the first ranks pay five hundred rupees,
the second three hundred, for opening the
ground ; and they are disjoined merely by
a broad road.

I intreated Mrs. Hartly would lead me to
my dear mother's last mansion—she started,
and accused herself of the highest indiscretion,
in consenting to my viewing a spot that could
suggest such an idea to my mind ; and so ear-
nestly besought me, as a proof of my affection for her, to return home, and never again
attempt to investigate a circumstance, so
evidently desired by my father to be kept
from my knowledge, that friendship and filial

reverence prevailed over every other impulse, and I suffered her to put me into my palanquin without reply.

But palanquins are conveyances ill calculated to remove distressing thoughts; and, during my state of miserable sequestration from all social connection, I would glad'y have exchanged places with any friend of yours, that enjoyed only a corner of a hackney-coach and your company. Nor shall I, from what I have this day experienced, ever be reconciled to this *sola* condition, however conformable to the fashion of the country. This letter, my dear girl, will waft a sigh from your

SOPHIA GOLDBORN.

LETTER XV.

HAVE I interested your curiosity by my mention of a concert? I can assure you, it well merits your notice and information.

It was performed in a grand hall or saloon, lofty and spacious beyond all I could have conceived. Dryden's *Timotheus* was one of the pieces with which we were presented:

the coronation Anthem a second, the overture to Artaxerxes, that *chef d'œuvre* of Arne, a third—of all which I was an inchanted auditor : yet there were moments, Arabella, when a painful pleasure, from the article of your absence, stole upon my heart, and traced out such correspondent lines in my countenance, that Mrs. Hartly (whom nothing escapes) charged me with some soft recollections of England. "Why will you not be sincere," said she, "with a woman whose heart is in your hand ; and confess, what is so apparent, that your affections are not your own ? Think you, I am not sufficiently liberal-minded to love those you love, and resign you, though one of the first pleasures of my existence, to the man of your choice ?—O wherefore is he an inhabitant of a world I must never hope to behold again ?"

Now, who shall say, that love and friendship are not the same ?—for similar are the sensations of the tender regret separation excites, and similar the animated delight of a reunion : and we shall meet, my Arabella, we shall re-enjoy the satisfactions distance deprives us of ; we shall—but all this plaintive language is very unoriental, and shall be renounced , and more especially, as there is no due proportion between the strength of your attachment and mine—for I follow the fortunes of my father—the hand of destiny has torn me from you : whereas you are now, on the death of your aunt, perfectly mistress of yourself, and can, if your inclination prompts you, come to me with propriety ; whereas I could not come to you, unaccompanied by my only parent, without dishonour—the dishonour of violating my filial duty. Let me hear from you on this point ; and take care you well acquit yourself, or, on being weighed in the usual balance of even my warmest partiality, you will be found wanting.

The Governor's dress gives you his character at once—unostentatious and sensible. His lady, however, is the great ornament of places of polite resort ; for her figure is elegant—her manner lively and engaging—and her whole appearance a model of taste and magnificence.

Envy, malice, and uncharitableness—how do those malign vices, blemish and deform that last best work of Heaven, the human mind ! —Perfection itself is not secure from their baneful breath. But I forget, upon this occasion, that there is a spur to their intent at Calcutta, beyond what they can generally plead. A change of Governor would introduce a change in Eastern politics ; and numbers blaze forth, that are now unremembered. But, as I have told you before, I am no judge of these matters ; and will not, therefore, trust myself on a subject that might mislead me. The heart will, I grant you, have its private decision, and its private election ; and what power or fiat, less than divine, shall deprive it of its natural rights ?

I foresaw that this concert would produce some great event. My father looked almost as young as his daughter ;—a circumstance I premise as an apology for what is to follow. A widow lady with thousands at her feet—a superior offer to every thing my youth and person has procured me—has insinuated, in so many very explicit terms, to Mrs. Hartly, that she is ambitious to make him master of them.

Mrs. Hartly executed her commission with a very grave face, and I laughed ; but, I believe, looked chagrined, on my father professing himself much honoured, and that he would wait upon the lady. Arabella, what do those

words imply ? that I have lost my father ?—
Was he not wedded to my mother's memory
when in England, when whole oceans rolled
between him and her hallowed remains ? and
can he, will he insult —But I have done : we
are none of us angels, my dear girl—we are
frail, frail mortality.

But should it be possible for so astonishing
an event to take place, farewell India, farewell
for ever ! My father's blessing, his permission
to end my days with you, and once, but once,
to behold my mother's tomb, is all I will ask :
for my grandfather, you know, has left me a
sufficient provision ; and I will constitute it
my sole support. My mind, so little power
have I over it, although I write so calmly, is
all a chaos.—My father calls for me : I will
instantly attend him—receive his commands
with firmness, with resignation ; nor dare so
far to invert the order of things, as to hope or
wish he should regulate his conduct by my
will and pleasure. He is my father, Arabella ;
and I have only to forget he was the husband
of my mother, to approve all his conduct.

The trial is over, and you shall judge how
I supported it, without one anticipating reflection escaping me. I found him alone

in the garden veranda, and unusually serious. He rose when I entered—smiled—and looked my father.

"My dear Sophy, " said he, seating both me and himself— "I am this instant returned from a very affecting scene." I sighed, and was silent.

"You heard what Mrs. Hartly said last night, and must recollect my reply." It was the nearest of all remembrances to my heart; but I only bowed in answer. " The lady, " continued he, "has a noble mind"— (I trembled as he spoke, but he was too much taken up with his subject to notice it)— " she deserved every polite attention in return for the high compliment she made me—and all things are settled between us. " "My mother!" exclaimed I, in a scarce articulate voice, and fainted in his arms—a fine piece of heroism, after all my preparation and re-solves! I instantly revived, complained of heat, and begged he would proceed.

"You are sensible, my beloved girl, " said he, "how awkward the situation of a young unmarried woman is at Calcutta;—you have declined every overture made you, though some of them deserved a better fate; but your inclinations are your own—I am the friend, not the tyrant of your heart, Sophia ; and such I will prove myself. ''

Ah ! sighed that rebellious heart—am I to be the saving consideration for your conduct ?

"A woman of honour, fortune, and merit,'' continued he, " is not an offer a man of my time of life could have thought of ; and the opportunity of giving my child a protector of her own sex, is an opportunity not to be left unimproved. She will not return to England without you ; and, with a greatness of soul you will respect, has transferred her affections from the father to the child.—Yes, my Sophia, she reveres my sorrows—acknowledges my heart cannot be recalled from the mansions of the dead—asks only my friendship, your friendship, and will prove an ornament to her sex. Our inclinations, I repeat it, will not always obey our voice ; whence I shall ever leave my child's unfettered :—but, though we cannot bestow them, we can regulate them at will, and make an act of stern necessity an act of choice, in every thing but delivering up our persons to an unbeloved object. ''

I wept aloud, Arabella—embraced my father—besought his pity and his pardon ;

and all this without his discovering my motive—for, unconscious of deviating in a single
thought from what was excellent and amiable
in his own character, it never once occurred
to him, that little mean suspicions occupied
my breast.

We are to dine with her to-morrow ; and
next to Mrs. Hartly, I have assured my father
I will love and revere her : but, from knowing
Mrs. Hartly first, she has got possession, said
I, of the very next place to my Arabella in my
affections, and I do think can never be super-
seded. My father smiled at my mental etiquette, and left me with a full purse to collect
myself at leisure.

Well do I now know my father is incapable
of changing :—but beware, Mrs. D——, how
you flatter, lest you should deceive yourself ;
for such a friend, Arabella, as my father must
be dangerous to such a heart as Mrs. D—'s ;
which, having once loved to the height of re-
vealing its sentiments—of rising superior to
the bars of decorum, and the chains of custom
—cannot answer for its feelings, or in future
hope to restrain them by any human fiat.
Yet hopeless love, my father says, where
the principles are pure and upright, always

subsides into friendship : it may be so ; but I would not chuse to adopt Mrs. D——'s example in this instance however unexceptionable I may find her in every other. Is this a mark of a narrow or a liberal way of thinking ? I will take your word for it, though I cannot my father's : he is no judge in his own cause, and entertains too great an opinion of the force of just sentiments and the authority of reason.

This is an eastern adventure we had not taken into our account :—but all females do not come under our British bard's description,

> ——— She never told her love,
> But let concealment, &c., &c.

for who does not know the lines as well as I, the writer of this epistle ? and it is impertinent to assume the credit of information we cannot give.

I shall to-morrow morning exchange the soft passion for the subjects I have till now uninterruptedly pursued——my accounts of Calcutta, etc., etc.

Your own
S G

LETTER XVI.

WEDDINGS here, Arabella, are very joyous things to all parties ; especially I should suppose, to the padre or clergyman, who frequently receives twenty gold mohrs for his trouble of performing the ceremony. The bride and bridegroom's friends assemble, all elegantly dressed, at one or other of the young couple's nearest relatives, and are most sumptuously entertained ; and the congratulatory visits on the occasion put the whole town in motion. It is a festival I have not, however, the smallest desire to treat my friends with ; for, even was my choice fixed, and every obstacle obviated, I should have unconquerable objections to making so public an exhibition of myself on so solemn a change of condition—an idea I cannot say I have in common with my acquaintance ; for I have reason to believe, I am the only person in Calcutta, not even my well-beloved Mrs. Hartly excepted, that has the same idea in this instance—which is entirely the effect of custom.

A very pleasing because a very singular circumstance, is, that in this country the head gardener is a professed botanist, and of course

conversible on every part of creation around
him : hence the classes and characters, as well
as the beauties, of those shrubs and flowers
that attract my notice most, are my frequent
topics of observation and enquiry. And
besides the entertainment, the benefit is
abundant of having a well-educated person in
this capacity ; for his judgment is the household land, where the garden is concerned ;
and you are sure to have your table supplied,
and your flower vases furnished with good
sense and propriety. Moreover, I can mention ladies, (and myself, Arabella, for one) who
when at a loss for a subject, are enabled, by
this gentleman's assistance, to read a lecture
on the several articles of which their bouquet
is composed. But to be serious, to me it is
highly agreeable, let the art or science be what
it may, to meet with people of information and
good address : it is giving you a companion
wherever you go, and promoting that disposition for local enjoyment so much recom-
mended by moral writers, and which undeni-
ably forms a large portion of our happiness.
Accordingly, I have already learned to distinguish the native and exotic beauties of the
parterre, and with no small pleasure (I might

say pride, for I certainly have much nationality about me) discover that many English plants and trees, particularly apple-trees, which are hard to rear, and consequently their fruit of great value, are treated with all the attention and tenderness foreign products are honoured with in England.

Besides, do but conceive the advantage to a man or woman of fashion, who has taste without leisure, and a desire of knowledge without the smallest inclination for study, to have a liberal-bred officer (I may properly call it) of their household, capable of qualifying them to figure away upon subjects that are an honour to human nature, with whom they can converse at will, on the most rational and delightful topics. If you love me, fail not to enforce these considerations on your wealthy and right honourable friends, and at least put them in possession of one means of shining. Nevertheless, my sweet friend, amidst all the joys our double seasons yield, the following lines frequently occur to me; and, if you can feel their truth in Britain, conceive how strongly they must affect my mind in this all subduing climate

Who can unpitying see the flow'ry race,
Shed by the morn, their new-flush'd bloom resign
Before the parching beam ?

Three of the gentlemen, who so largely con-
tributed to our entertainment at the concert,
are, I find, theatrical performers ; the Patty
and Miss Sycamore of the Maid of the
Mill, the Rosetta and Lucinda of Love in a
Village ; and such are their agreeable persons, that I doubt not but, by the aids of
the toilet, they fill up those several parts
without dissatisfaction to either the ear
or eye.

I have not yet described to you the wonders of a dessert. Ices, Arabella, (could you
have supposed such a thing ?) ices, in the highest perfection, are, in the months of November and December, presented you at Calcutta.
—This circumstance of the ice was to me so
wonderful, that I was earnest to have it accounted for ; and I find, that this temporary
luxury is procured from some of the slender
inland (if I may so express myself) branches
of the Ganges, which are cut out into canals,
or flow in rivulets, under various names. A
thin plate of ice forming itself thereon, in some
of the coldest nights the coldest season affords,

is taken from thence with great care, and manufactured for the first tables : nor do some of the tanks or fish-ponds less advance the purposes of elegant accommodation in this respect, when the evenings are such as you have in April, or the mornings somewhat like your month of October.

At supper last night I drank a glass of ex- cellent London porter, with sensations of re- cognition you may much better imagine than I can describe. Mrs. Hartly tells me, it is always on the sideboard, for those who like it ; but I never before heard it mentioned. We have also small-beer, perry, and cyder, from my native country, and fine spruce-beer, the produce of Bengal ; and, having more company than usual, we did not retire until after four o'clock : and I begin almost to think it just, that those who thus continue to have two days in one, should live but half as long as those people who divide their existence, upon even a fashionable average, between sleep and amusement.

Had Thomson never been in India, how, let me ask you, could he have so admirably described an animal, that, to be known in all its terrors, must be seen ?

Lo ! the green serpent, from its dark abode,
Which e'en Imagination fears to tread,
At noon forth issuing, gathers up its train
In orbs immense, then, darting out anew,
Seeks the refreshing fount ; by which diffus'd
He throws his folds : and, while with threat'ning tongue,
And deathful jaws erect, the monster curls
His flaming crest, all other thirst, appall'd,
Or shiv'ring flies, or check'd at distance stands,
Nor dares approach.

To-morrow I am to be presented to
Mrs. D—. I feel an awkwardness, I know not
why ; for, from the accounts I have received
of her, any other worthy man but my own
dear father should have my warmest vote to
obtain her. Her fortune, Arabella, is her
smallest merit ; for she possesses, it seems,
much intellectual cultivation, and has an excellent heart ;—a *soft* one she has proved it
to be. Good-night : read not the last two or
three lines with attention, that you may not
condemn

Your most affectionate,

S. G.

LETTER XVII.

THE visit is over—and, if my father can resist the merits and winning graces of this woman, I will only say, he is more than human.

Ah! Arabella, with what nice attention had she prepared for our reception!—her house is a palace in miniature, and her servants the best-formed and disciplined, if I may so express myself, I have ever yet seen.

I approached her with a somewhat of awe and reserve I could not get the better of ; but her countenance is open as day, and her smile engaging.—"By permission, Madam," said my father, with an air of humility I am confident touched her to the soul, "by your permission I bring my daughter to solicit your friendship ; she is prepared to honour you, and your indulgence will soon teach her to love you ; and may this first interview be ever remembered by you both with the pleasure it gives to me."

"You have deceived me, Sir," said she —"Is it this child, that stands in need of countenance and support ? What may she not command at Calcutta! She exceeds my utmost expectation.''

"Sophia," replied he, "is a good girl, Madam, and has continued to lay her father under the greatest obligations; her voyage to India was solely for my sake; she has left friendships behind her that are not easily supplied: it is incumbent upon me, therefore, to procure her every possible compensation.''

A polite and animated return was made by the lady to this speech, and perfectly became her; for, as she does not call herself young, she has a licence to speak in terms that would be too assuming for you or me. But I have a discovery to communicate, that alarms me, perhaps without a cause;—she has a son, Arabella; and, as their heads at Calcutta are full of lovers and husbands, I am more than half afraid there is some plot in this sudden acquaintance and friendship.

I watched her eyes with diligence; but her whole demeanor was unexceptionable, and the character of the fair friend finely preserved; but she seems to understand the method of attaching such a man as my father, and, I fear will reserve the fable of the Turtle and Ring Dove having got the clue from him to his heart, by making herself as necessary to his peace, as she must be pleasing to his sensibility.

Now, Arabella, am I about to play the woman in a most unworthy degree. I have never beheld Mrs. D—'s son, or even heard of him until this visit ; yet am I armed, at all points, to refuse an offer I may never receive. —What unpardonable prejudgment ! May he not have his mother's graces, his mother's understanding, which is much celebrated ? He may ; but take my word for it, he is not the man I shall ever unite myself to ; for your made-up matches are, of all things, the most odious to me. Let the man have eyes to chuse me, on whom I am ever prevailed upon to bestow my hand, that I may not suppose the question is coolly canvassed whether I shall be accepted by him, aye or no. I am neither a vain nor ambitious woman ; but I own I am not able to stand the idea of being pointed out by the maternal finger to a booby heir, that would never otherwise have thought of me. I would not thus be disposed of, even to the Nabob himself. Jerry Blackacre (for so my mind would perversely call this unknown young man) never once, however,

made his appearance ; nor did Mamma glance
the way I apprehended. May I find myself
alarmed without a cause !

Mrs. D——is a 'woman of taste and good
education, and has a menagery, as you call
it in England, of the feathered tribes peculiar
to this country ; beautiful cockatoos, and
minhos without number ; lories—but she gave
five-and-twenty gold mohrs for three of them ;
they are natives of Batavia, and in high esteem here for their articulation : she has also
a bird with buff-coloured wings and a white
breast, of the Bilo species, that has a million
of worshippers among the Gentoos, and
named by them the Bramine kite.

She has presented me with one of each if
Mrs. Hartly can forgive my introduction of
them into her family ; but I am certain if
they prove inconvenient inmates at Calcutta,
she will have them accommodated at Hartly
bungilo, and my little friends will be kind to
them for my sake.

There are, besides the Bramine kite, very
many birds that enjoy high privileges ; the
Indian raven, for example, (a bird known in
Europe by the name of the Rhinoceros bird)
which draw themselves up in curious ranks in

the most populous streets of this town without interruption, and are called by the sailors Jerry Daw's soldiers.

Mrs. D——is to return our visit in a few days. I am but a novice in these matters ; but it appears very extraordinary to me, that, after what has passed between her and Mrs. Hartly, (and that she cannot flatter herself my father's refusal of her can be a secret, as it speaks herself) she should chuse to mix with such heterogeneous parties : but she carries off the affair with an admirable grace, in which my father assists her in a manner peculiar to himself, and, I believe, without her perception of it. It is well for the world at large, and happy for me, that all his arts are honest ones, and all his frauds pious ; for, had a bad man his endowments, his collected mind, his command of face, who would be able to stand against him ? I will teach myself to be a more dutiful daughter, and less capricious member of the community, that I may merit the partiality I know you feel for

Your's etc.,
S. G.

LETTER XVIII.

No wonder lawyers return from this country, rolling in wealth ; their fees are enormous ; if you ask a single question on any affair, you pay down your gold mohr, Arabella, (two pounds) ! and if he writes a letter of only three lines, twenty-eight rupees (four pounds) ! I tremble at the idea of coming into their hands, for what must be the recoveries, to answer such immense charges !—You must, however; be informed, that the number of acting attornies on the court roll is restricted to twelve ; who serve an articled clerkship of three years only, instead of five, as in England. These twelve regular bred gentlemen nevertheless, from motives of friendships, or for certain *douceurs* best known to themselves, lend their names, on manifold occasions, to the great extension of practice.

The style of living, if you wish to be deemed genteel, is indeed such as demands an ample revenue ; but the custom of the country is so much in favour of improving your fortune at all points, that it is not considered in the smallest degree derogatory for gentlemen of whatever denomination to merchandise, or, as I

have already mentioned, to provide lodgings
or lodging-houses for the East India Company
servants, who are only temporary residents.

The fee for making a will is in proportion
to its length, from five gold mohrs upwards
and as to marriage articles, I should imagine
they would half ruin a man, and a process at
law be the destruction of both parties. A
man of abilities and good address in this line,
if he has the firmness to resist the fashionable
contagion, gambling, need only pass one seven
years of his life at Calcutta, to return home in
affluent circumstances ; but the very nature
of their profession leads them into gay
connections, and, having for a time complied
with the humour of their company from
prudential motives, they become tainted, and
prosecute their bane from the impulses of
inclination.

My father's Sekar has obliged me with
the introduction of his relation, the
young Bramin, at Hartly House. He has
not left the Gentoo university at Benares,
which is remarkable for its sanctity, above
three years. He made us, however, but a very
short visit ; as it was near our tea-hour, and
he could not by the laws of his religion,

partake of any refreshment ; but promised
by his interpreter to see us again soon. My
vanity will not let me suppress one compliment that was paid me by a Moor of
great dignity :

"Such," said he, "are the daughters of Para-
dise."——I would have given more than I
shall mention to have known my Bramin had
distinguished me from the rest of the company ; but was not so happy. We will, nevertheless, if you please, talk of him in his
absence, or at least of the people to which
he belongs.

The Gentoos, Arabella, are divided into
five tribes ; the first of which is the most highly esteemed, and the only one (like the tribe of
Levi among the Jews) from whence the priests
are taken : I need not therefore add, it is
called Bramins.

The second is the Sittris, whose profession
ought to be the military alone ; but they are
not so strict as the preceding, and frequently
engage in other employments.

The third are called the Beisa tribe, which
consist chiefly of merchants, bankers, and
banias or shop-keepers ; the sekars are, I
believe, of this tribe.

The fourth are called the Sudder tribe, who, by their original institution, are the meanest servants ; nor can they ever rise higher.

And the fifth are called Atarris, which is a tribe deserted by and formed of the refuse of all the others ; the travelling-palanquin-bearers, the most inferior and laborious of all offices, are taken from thence. And I will in this place inform you, that the travelling palanquins are so constructed, that you repose, as in Revel's machine, on a couch—are served with your loll shrub, or other favourite refreshments—and thus, with incredible expedition, are conveyed to the distance of five hundred, or any other number of miles, up the country ; and there is no other mode of travelling by land whatever.

By water, you have bugeros of so large a size as to accommodate whole families ; and, being provided wth live and other suitable stock to your fortune, etc., you shorten or lengthen your voyage at pleasure, and have your state-room cooled by verandas, as in your own houses. You will therefore perceive that our pleasures are not so local as might be imagined ; and, in these nautical excursions, it is common for several bugeros to set out in company, interchange their visits, and have their little concerts, as agreeably as may be. A party of this sort is planned for my participation, and I suppose Mrs. D——will be added to the list ; be it so ; but, if she would give me a favourable impression of her prudence, she will decline being in the same bugero with my father.

She has, however, told me some interesting things ; and I begin to have confidence in her friendship.

Her father and mother were both English, but she was born at Cacutta ; they conspired, Arabella, at a tender age, to sacrifice their child for wealth. A marriage (if it could be so called, that was a violence on the heart) was agreed to by them, when Mrs. D——was only twelve years old, with a great military character, whose manners were ferocious, and his person deformed. Nine years did he live, the tyrant and the oppressor of all who knew him. A library was the sole support of her spirits, and the sole relaxation she was permitted to enjoy. She bore all without complaint ; for she was sensible complaint would be unavailing. Her father and mother were little benefitted by their conduct; the man of

war forbad them all intercourse with his wife
—he would not have her taught the sin of opposition to his will; she was his property, and
as such he would guard her from the approach
of persons who had, to his knowledge, private
views to gratify : and at length, in order to
deliver himself from their reproaches, he offered them an annuity for life, on condition they
resided in England ; for England they embarked, without being allowed a parting interview with their child, but were lost in their
passage, on the Malabar coast ; which piece
of news her husband abruptly communicated
to her, and laughed at the tears it occasioned
her. "You could not love them, " said he,
" it is impossible ; the matrimonial sale they
made of you renders it impossible ;—to enrich themselves, they were wholly regardless
of your fate ; and, had you not married a
man of honour, you must have been miserable. "——He died, however, at the end of
nine years, and she has remained nine years
a widow.

Her fortune, it seems, has only a short time
been clear of litigation ; and her health,
during that whole period, was in a very indifferent state. The first is now ascertained to

her utmost satisfaction, and the second happily re-established ; when, unluckily, Arabella,
she has created a new grievance for herself,
that nothing but her own death, in all
probability, can deliver her from smarting
under.—But I will return to the Gentoos.

The Bramins pretend that Brumma, who
was their legislator both in politics and religion, was inferior only to God. He was,
possibly, some great and good genius, that, in
like manner with Confucius of the Chinese,
regulated their manners, and promoted their
happiness ; and is therefore rendered, by
gratitude and superstition, the object of
their adoration.

The Bramins, however, affirm that he be-
queathed them a book called the Vidam, containing all his doctrines and institutions ; and
that, though the original is lost, they are still
possessed of a commentary upon it, which
they name the Shahstah, written in the Shan-
scrita language ; a dead language at this time
and known only to the priests who study it.
The foundation of Brumma's doctrine consit-
ed, it is said, in the belief of a Supreme Being,
who created a regular gradation of beings,
some superior, and some inferior to man ;—

in the immortality of the soul ; and a future
state of rewards and punishments, to be bestowed and received in a transmigration into
different bodies, according to the lives they
had led in their pre-existent state. From
which it appears most likely that the Pythagorean metempsychosis took its rise in India ;——but that the necessity of inculcating
this sublime, but otherwise complicated doctrine, into the lower ranks, induced the priests,
who are by no means (the case in most religions
under the sun) unanimous in their doctrines,
to have recourse to sensible representations
of the Deity and his attributes : so that the
original doctrines of Brumma have degener-
ated into downright and ridiculous idolatry,
in the worship of divers animals, of a variety
of images, and some of the most hideous figures, either delineated or carved, and they
have holidays to the number of twenty annually, in honour of each;—a kind of religious
jubilee, during which public processions and
festivals take place ; which I shall not fail to
describe to you on becoming a spectator
of them.

All their other pleasures are confined to
visiting their pagodas, or temples, which are

stupendous but disgusting buildings, and to
the satisfactions of domestic life ; and they
assuredly are, as I have already observed to
you, the most tranquil and temperate people
on earth. But, besides the tribes I have set
before you——their ancient mode of arrang-
ing their precedence, and their numbers of
casts or classes, divisions of those tribes, I
shall have occasion to observe to you hereafter. Water is their drink ; but such, Arabella, is their strict adherence to what they
deem their religious duties, that though expiring with thirst, they would not taste the
water of their sacred rivers, the Indus, called
by them *Sindah*, the Kisna, and the Ganges ;
the tanks or fish-ponds, fed by the heavens,
or by natural springs, being alone their liquor
on all occasions. But they never fail to wash
themselves in the Ganges, or to oil their bodies,
before they break their fast. In a word,
their manners are highly interesting, from
their simplicity and liberal-mindedness ; and
I blush to feel how superior to all that Christianity can boast, of peace and good-will
towards men. But, my dear Arabella, I have
one caution to give you, which is, not to set
me down for a plagiarist, though you should

even stumble upon the likeness, verbatim, of
my descriptions of the Eastern world in print ;
at once presume to consider such printed
accounts as other than honourable testimonies
of my faithful relations : and certain it is, that
true and genuine relations of objects and events
admit of very little variation of language.
This premised, I shall not doubt of informing
or entertaining you (and perhaps both the
one and the other) in repeated instances ; and
ill requited be the busy individual that attempts to lessen the consequence, or impeach
the originality of my reports.

This doctrine of the metempsychosis is to
me the religion of humanity ; for it is apparent,
that no other tenet, temporal or divine, could
have so effectually restrained the sons and
daughters of this Eastern world from commit-
ting the wantonest acts of cruelty towards
the brute creation, as the apprehension of
being exposed, by the chances of transmigration, to similar evils ;—apparent from the
marking effect it has on the conduct of the
Gentoos, in contradistinction to all other
species of natives ; for, instead of the arrogance
and ferocity daily manifested by the several
nations around them, their hearts are softened

into a tender concern for the kind treatment of every creature living—a concern which so powerfully regulates their feeling, that, in the very bosom of voluptuousness, they will feed on no delicacies but such as the vegetable kingdom presents them with, except the nectareous juices obtainable from animals with relief to themselves, and salubrity to their owners—a very elegant manner, I expect you to allow, of telling you that milk is a favourite article of the Gentoo diet. How unlike the degenerate posterity of Adam

(Of half that live, the butcher and the tomb)

in this order of beings ! and how easy the transition into angelic natures !

But enough of the Gentoos for the present, and of every other subject, except the last and first that occupies my thoughts, namely, with what affection I am,

Your unalterable friend, etc., etc.,
S. G.

LETTER XIX.

PHYSIC, as well as law, is a gold mine to its professors, to work it at will. The medical gentlemen at Calcutta, Arabella, make their visits in palanquins, and receive a gold mohr each patient, for every common attendance —extras are enormous.

Medicines are also rated so high, that it is shocking to think of : in order to soften which public evil as much as possible, an apothecary's shop is opened at the Old Fort, by the Company, in the nature of your London dispensaries, where drugs are vended upon reasonable terms. The following charges are a specimen of the expences those Europeans incur, who sacrifice to appearances.

An ounce of bark, three rupees, seven and sixpence—an ounce of salts, one rupee, half a crown—a bolus, one rupee—a blister, two rupees, five shillings—and so on in proportion ; so that, literally speaking, you may ruin your fortune to preserve your life.

But then, to balance this formidable account, every profession has its amazing advantages : accordingly, as I am told, it is no uncommon thing to clear 140 per cent. by merchandize

on many European articles, and particularly
the ornamental for ladies, and on men's hats.

Moreover, from the high demands at
taverns and coffee houses, you may conclude
provisions are brought to market at a high
price : on the contrary, even during the time
the East India Company's ships are lying off
Calcutta, and so abundantly increase the consumption, six fine ducks are sold for a rupee,
two and sixpence. Bread is also good and
cheap ; fish both excellent and cheap. Like-
wise fowls, eggs, and milk, very cheap;
butter dear—geese cheap—turkies dear ; and
Arabella, half a sheep is often bought for
one rupee. Vegetables are plentiful and very
fine—the potatoes are better tasted, in my
opinion, though much smaller, than in their
native soil—we have salads in great quantities, and within every one's purchase—and
French beans and green pease, are, I am told,
in as high perfection at Christmas, as in the
meridian of your summer season, and with
this advantage, that they have them in your
summer also. Fruit of every kind is delightful—oranges, lemons, limes, pomegranates,
bananas, pommelos (which are brought to
table stript of their outside coat), plantains,

etc., etc., the product of their own soil ; with
apples, as a rarity, currants, raspberries, etc.
etc., from my native country, and raised here
with much care and attention. Thus you will
perceive wine is the heaviest family article ;
for, whether it is taken fashionably or
medicinally, every lady, even to your humble
servant, drinks at least a bottle *per diem*, and
the gentlemen four times that quantity—a
fine number of twelve and sixpences in the
course of the year ! Their domestic animals
are the same as in England—and, in like manner with England, dogs of various kinds, and
cats are great favourites—the ladies have
also parrots, squirrels, minhos, lories, etc.,
etc., as pets.

They have elephants, camels, horses (Arabian and Armenian), oxen, buffaloes, sheep,
deer, lions, and

> Tigers darting fierce
> Impetuous on the prey their glance has doom'd.

as Thomson tells you ; with many I have not
enabled myself to mention. Nor must you
be uninformed, that to hunt this terrific creature, is one of the polite amusements of the
East ; on which occasion the gentlemen set
forth with all imaginable magnificence, with

bands of music, and dogs, and spears, and
sometimes give fatal displays of their courage.
I am happy to know my father will never
make one in such wild parties ; for surely
there is much more of madness than folly, in
thus sporting with their personal safety, and
braving the author of their existence. I know
very well, Arabella, that hunting these rapa-
cious and powerful animals, can boast both
ancient and regal origin ; but what is wrong
in itself, can never be rendered right, because
some illustrious brute or blockhead has made
it his practice.

The farmers, who supply the Calcutta
markets, reside chiefly about creeks and little
bays formed by the artificial meanders of the
Ganges—and have a Beisar day once a week,
for the sale of their commodities—especially
up Tomluck river, as high as eight miles,
which, though shallow, is navigable for all
Bugeros ; and it is fashionable to visit the
dairies, etc., etc., in its neighbourhood.

Confectionary shops are kept both by
French and English men ; but the latter are
most approved, and their profits are far from
inconsiderable—nor is it unreasonable it should
be so, when it is remembered they have their

wishes to revisit the country of their birth, in common with their superiors ; and are willing to purchase that felicity by dint of toil, in the service of those who choose to employ them : they have large imports in this way, as, I believe, I have already mentioned, from England. You will perceive I am not unobserving or unenquiring. But to proceed to other matters. His Majesty's Coronation would have been ushered in with ringing of bells (the constant herald of joy in England) but for one little impediment, *viz*., Arabella, there is but one church bell at present in Calcutta, and a deep melancholy-toned one, for the sole purpose of telling the public some one of their fellow individuals is no more. All funeral processions are however concealed as much as possible from the sight of the ladies, that the vivacity of their tempers may not be wounded.

Funerals are indeed solemn and affecting things at Calcutta, no hearses being here introduced, or hired mourners employed : for, as it often happens in the gay circles, that a friend is dined with one day, and the next in eternity—the feelings are interested, the sensations awful, and the mental question, for the

period of interment at least, "which will be
to-morrow's victim ?''—The departed one, of
whatever rank, is carried on men's shoulders
(like your walking funerals in England) and a
procession of gentlemen equally numerous,
and respectable from the extent of genteel con-
nexions, following—the well-situated and the
worthy being universally esteemed and car-
essed whilst living, and lamented when dead.
The Padra, however, has his ample profits;
who performs this last pious act with the
greatest propriety : but such is the elasticity
of European minds, that, the ensuing day,
the tavern is again visited by those very gentlemen, who know, and acknowledge it to have
been the bane of their lost friend—excesses
of this kind being only suicide in a different
form than the pistol or sword, by which many
of my country men in England precipitate
themselves into the mansion of spirits, with
how much confusion of heart and of face, no one
has yet been permitted to return and declare;
—but they have reason and morality for their
guide, and when those are unattended to, it is
not probable they would be made sensible of
the first law and duty of existence, self-pre-
servation, though one rose from the dead.

As a relieving subject, however, both for you and myself, I will mention to you, on this opportunity, somewhat of christenings :—five gold mohrs is the smallest fee thought of for the Padra's trouble in this instance—with the participation, moreover, of an entertainment that would put a lord mayor's festival out of countenance : his Reverence must therefore have a fine time of it ;—but gold mohrs are dealt about at Calcutta, as half crowns in England ; and I leave you to determine with how good a grace a family of fortune or title could offer a clerical man, of respectable character, half a crown for his baptismal benediction.

The Gentoo holidays begin to-morrow—when I suppose I shall have news for you ; and you may assure yourself I shall be on the look out to do you pleasure.

I have seen the opening procession, and am much entertained by it. A certain number of Bramins, dressed after their peculiar manner with countenances such as Guido would have bestowed on a heavenly saint, led the way, prodigious multitude of people following, with an idol superbly dressed with silver, gold, pearls, and the richest manufactures—

which is carried about from street to street,
till sufficiently exhibited, with drums, flutes,
etc., etc., to the manifest delight of all parties, and then lodged in one of their pagodas
as a sacred, though temporary, deposit; for
it seems, Arabella, that on the last day of
these religious raree-shews, all the idols are
collected into a body, and, in a kind of pious
frenzy, plunged into the Ganges, with thirty
or forty persons swimming round them, until
the noble act of sinking them to the bottom
is effected, when they return with inconceiv-
able satisfaction to their respective homes—
and then proper persons are set to work to
furnish them with new ones; the poor delud-
ed creatures endangering their lives, though
most expert swimmers; for the contest is,
who shall be the happy one to perform this
ceremony, conceiving it the highest honour
of mortality to be aiding and assisting in drown-
ing these divine works of their own hands.

It is, indeed, one of the grand articles of
the Gentoo faith, that the waters of the
rivers Ganges, Kisna, and Indus, have the sacred virtue of purifying those who bathe
therein, from all pollutions and sins—they are
therefore commanded by Brumma, (in his

book of pious instructions, the Vidam) to dwell
solely in the neighbourhood of some one of
them—a tenet that is founded in good policy,
by its prohibition of their migrating into distant countries; for it is remarkable, that the
sacred rivers are so situated, that there is no
part of India where the inhabitants have not
an opportunity of freeing themselves from their
sins by this mode of purgation;—the Ganges
flowing through the kingdom of Bengal—the
Kisna dividing the Carnatic from Golconda and
the Sindale, or Indus washing Gugurate, and
all the parts bordering upon Persia.—But they
do not want any thing from abroad, having
neither vanity nor ambition to gratify.

They are subject to early old age, as I have
mentioned on a former occasion; and have so
little passion for vigorous exertions, that it
is a favourite maxim with them, That it is
better to sit than to walk, to lie down than
to sit, to sleep than to wake, and that death
is best of all.

So soon as these holidays are over, the races
will take place, and I am preparing to appear
with *eclat* as my father's daughter.—I cost him
large sums; but we cannot have the purchase
without the price; and, I promise you, he has

the full credit of his generosity to me.—He
calls me his second self—I think he miscalls
me, for I verily believe I am the first object
of his care and kindness ; nay more, that he is
attentive to his own health and accommodation, chiefly on my account—and I with very
many young women, more deserving than
myself, could say the same.

I have as yet given you only a very inade-
quate idea of the wealth, the numerous dependents, the power, and the importance of
the Company on this commercial spot.—However, before I advance one step further, let
me set before you the rapid progress they have
made in all these acquisitions.

In the year 1600, their stock consisted of
only £70,000—they nevertheless had the spirit
to fit out four ships, which being sucessful,
their prosperity augmented annually.

East India Company stock sold from 360
to 500 per cent. in 1680—and a new company
was established in 1689—the old one re-established, and the two united, in 1700—and they
agreed to give Government £400,000 a year, for
four years, to remain uninterrupted, in 1769.

Such are the prosperous flights of commerce,
when wisdom and justice holds the regulat-

ing rein ;——but there are Phaetons every where ; and no wonder, therefore, that this chariot of the sun has had its wheels taken off at certain periods. Temptation is the fiery ordeal of virtue, and eastern bribes so portaable, that it is almost a miracle to escape unhurt in some tender part—our fame or our conscience ;—and let him that is qualified stand forth, and prove he is not included under this description of men.

I enquire every day about the arrival of ships, and find many do arrive ; whence comes it then, Arabella, that you remember me not ?

Mrs. Hartly has looked in upon me, and most severely condemns my close application to my pen.—I shall blind myself, she says, and tear my nerves to pieces.—She found me not only incorrigible, but I set such good and sufficient reasons before her, for the practice she impeached, that she left me, (having given me the information, that the races commence in three days) confessing it could not be discontinued. In three days, therefore, my dear Arabella, you attend me to the turf, where, if I do not break forth on the public eye with unusual spirit, I greatly fear the celebrity I can now boast will attain its utmost meridian and rapidly decline : the preparation is important, and my friends must be consulted in every instance—I therefore beg leave to devote this whole day, at least, to the advancement of so great and necessary a design, without writing another word.

Here you have me again, beyond my own promise or intention, engaged in your service ; —but, you must know, I have met with a little surprise of a singular nature—an addition, Arabella, to our usual visitants.—— I therefore said not a word respecting my appearance, but waited in quiet expectation of the young man's being announced to me, (as is the custom) previous to every notice I could condescend to take of him.

The morning passed away, and he was not announced !—strange this—but true—— if he is deemed worthy admission to our parties, why should he not have the usual passport to conversation ?—But it is idle for me to mention such a circumstance—and yet, as he appeared a stranger, and has a face of promise (for it is only doing him justice to say understanding and good-nature are apparent in his countenance), I must think it wrong to leave me in my awkward situation respecting him. If Mrs. Hartly thinks I shall make him of so much consequence as to enquire after him, she is mistaken; for I am too well aware of the inference, as it is the first thing of the kind that could be charged upon me, —I will order my palanquin, and steal a visit to the children I so much admire—their kind and innocent endearments will be doubly agreeable to me, now that I am in an absolute fit of dishumour with myself, and all the world—you, Arabella, alone excepted; my father, on this occasion, having shewn no more attention to my feelings, than the rest of my friends in this house.

So said, and so done—for, Arabella, before a single creature had an idea of such a thing, was I arrived at Hartly Bungilo, and as happy as a princess. Mrs. Rider, the children's *governante*, received me in a most pleasing manner; and I for the first time, had leisure to observe a custom, with which I am delighted —it is the compliment paid to my country, in the taste at Calcutta in statuary; for instead of Neptune, his lady wife, and whole train of aquatic attendants, saluting your eye, out of their natural element, these Bungilo gardens are adorned by a Thomson, a Johnson,

etc., etc., in a word, all the literary characters to which the British empire has given
birth ; and a very useful effect those objects have upon the mind—for, by a natural
and instantaneous combination of ideas, the
Seasons were opened on my view ; with Ras-
selas and his friends I traversed the Ethiopian
regions ; and so of the rest : nor did I ever,
until that moment, know the fund of literary
knowledge I am mistress of : and the utility
must be general to the beholders ;—for in
youth it excites enquiry, in maturity, recollection : and it is my fixt and firm resolve,
whenever I revisit England, (a nabobess,
you will observe) to constitute my gardens
an equal source of entertainment and instruc-
tion to all who are permitted to frequent them.
—Mrs. Rider, perceiving how enthusiastic I
was become, (for I absolutely answered her
kind and polite questions in heroics) said she
was tempted to shew me Mrs. Hartly's closet
—"Your visits, Madam," continued she,
"have been so short, that I conceived there
was not time to introduce you, where you
would doubtless wish to spend some hours—
for it is a cabinet of no less elegant than rational curiosities, and I have the honour to be

trusted with the key, for the purpose of improving the minds of my young pupils, as occasion requires, with little lectures upon its contents.'' I was impatient to be admitted; and the obliging Mrs. Rider led the way, without further preface or preparation.

I will never forgive Mrs. Hartly, for so long keeping me unacquainted with this proof of her fine taste, liberality of temper, admirable judgment, and elegant mode of spending her leisure time. The walls are covered with a pink paper from China, of the softest tint, as a ground to the portraits arranged around.— Here, Arabella, the poor Marchioness of Tavistock, from the hands of one of your first artists, sheds her unavailing tears, the tears of conjugal affection and wounded peace, never more to be healed on this side the mansions of eternity. And here also the lovely and royal victim of female ambition, is drawn in her state of disconsolation, robbed of her crown, her fame, her children, of all that is dear and estimable in existence, except her beauty—but that is pourtrayed in a style of languor and softness, that relieves the feelings, by intimating her sufferings are near their termination. Ah! my Arabella, who lost

more, or had more to lose, than this sweet
child of sorrow—transplanted from the nursery
to a throne, and surrounded by dangers,
against which she had never been taught
to guard—the malign dangers of self-interest
in a high-reaching and daring breast! But
I shall take an opportunity of speaking more
largely on the subject, as also giving you the
names of the other fair and amiable person-
ages, selected by my distinguishing friend
from all others to ornament and embellish
this invaluable, apartment. One more, however, I must place before you—a whole
length ; a highly finished piece—inscribed,
Arabella, thus,

> " Whose nice discernment Virgil-like, is such,
> **Never** to say too little, or too much."

The drapery is well executed, the attitude
happily chosen, the likeness masterly ; the
commentary on the *Genius of Shakespear*,
which lies on a table in the back-ground, a
very pleasing termination of the whole.

I own, I feel myself proud, when my mind
tells me this lady is my country-woman ; for to
her literary endowments are superadded gifts,
that bespeak her one of the first favourites

of Heaven—a heart replete with benevolence, and a hand prompt to bestow ; in a word she is an equal honour and blessing to the age in which she lives.

Mrs. Rider hinted to me (with great deference) that I should make my friends uneasy by my elopement ; and, my father having a right to my unremitting attention, however, I might chose to fancy he neglected me, I hesitated not to return ;—where I found the family in amazement, and the young gentleman seemed to have adopted their feelings. I laughed the matter off with a good grace, and, professing myself infinitely obliged to Mrs. Rider, for her entertainment of me, retired, and was not again visible till supper.

At supper the races was the universal topic, —and I find English jockies are well rewarded if they visit Calcutta. There will be a ball on the evening of the first day, given by the Company, at the Court-house, to which all the Company's servants are entitled to free admission. So that, at least, there will be men enough ; and, as the weather is remarkably favourable, fine sport is expected. Thus, you find, we Asiatics can contrive to vary our pleasures ; and must be the envy of the

European ladies, were they to read that we of Calcutta live only to be adored, and that our gentlemen ask no higher happiness than permission to pay us their unending adoration. You shall hear of me again in a few hours —at five o'clock in the afternoon we take our phaetons. The race-ground is three miles in circuit, and, I imagine, is found a laborious heat in this country, for once round is all that is attempted. But I will not prejudge an exhibition, of which I shall so soon become a glad spectator :—the horses are bred and attended at a great expence, as with you in England. But I have done—adieu !

LETTER XX.

Four in the morning.

I AM so delighted, and so fatigued—have so much to communicate, but, unlike your heroines in romance, am so unable to keep myself awake—that the moment my musketo curtains are ready, I must slide into repose ; and may the dreams of the morning

only equal the pleasures of the evening, and
I shall not, except in your absence, have a
wish ungratified.

I promised to address you again on paper
yesterday ; but I little foresaw what business
was in store for me. Mrs. D—, as I imagined,
goes with us, and came last night, at a
late hour, to solicit Mr. Hartly's company
in her phaeton I looked at my father—
who, turning to Mrs. Hartly, said, "I hope
you understand, Madam, that I rely upon the
honour of being your attendant beau on
every public pleasurable occasion." Mrs.
Hartly bowed, and smiled assent.

There sat the stranger speechless, though
animated—and, until I had refused several
gay offers, spoke not ; when, in a half whisper
the spirit at length moved him to ask, if he
might aspire—and a look of meaning was
left to finish the sentence.

My father said he should be most happy,
and Mrs. Hartly was warm in his recommendation—I, therefore, could not decline an
offer, I nevertheless scarcely knew how to
accept, as he remained the John in the
cloud every body is deemed until they are
introduced.

Having opened his mouth for the first time, in my presence, with success, he began to take a part in the conversation ; and I soon discovered two things—yes, Arabella, two, unless I am greatly deceived, namely, that he is a well-bred youth, and not without the secret desire of becoming one of my most obedient humble servants. But my obedient humble servants are already so numerous, that I do not believe I have room for one more upon the list. I nevertheless think you would plead in his behalf, if you was to see him : he is—so in fact like yourself in his person, has so agreeable a voice, so happy a manner, and fifty other valuable accomplishments, that, was I in a land where love was of longer duration before it terminates in matrimony, I will not say but I might be in some danger of listening to him ;—but such is the custom at Calcutta, that, before I shall be certain my affections are really engaged, or that I am likely to be able to prevail on myself to fix for life, he will be snapped up, if he has brought an unengaged heart among us, (which is to me, however, a doubtful point) by some female or other, who regulates both her feelings and her conduct by the established standard.

I shall, therefore, enter into nothing more than
a very slight acquaintance with him. But
the races, perhaps, you ask—when are you to
hear of the races ?

In the first place, Arabella, allow me to tell
you, (for it is a proper prelude to what follows)
not a phaeton on the turf was more noticed
than mine—my horses are Armenian, well
trained and bitted—my reins elegant—my
own dress becoming——the dress of my Seapoys magnificent—my attendant beau the
envy of the men, and the admiration of the
women :—and could any happiness be more
complete than mine ?

My father, however, played the renegade,
and exchanged his place in the phaeton, with
a gentleman on horseback :—he generally
kept near us his eyes, what paternal approbation did they not sparkle with ! though
he seemed to forbid their saying too much ;
and my beau had a dignity in his visible
satisfaction, that proved him to be of European birth and education—of taste and senti·
ment. For, however, little he said, he was
to me the best male companion I have met
with at Calcutta, the Governor and Mr.
Hartly excepted.

The spectators were numerous—many of which were Moors ; and observe, Arabella, (though that piece of information is in no degree connected with my present subject) that the Moors of Indostan, often called Mongols, are of the faith of Omar, the Turkish Mahometans of the faith of Hali.

The horses were led to the starting chair, four in number ; and the jockies, distinguished by the colour of their turbans, prepared themselves for the word of command—the word, Arabella, was given, and they went off full speed—my eyes followed them, not wholly impartially, for my father had declared his wishes, and his wishes were adopted by me. Our favourite was the successful adventurer ; but, between ourselves, such are the disadvantages of climate, that one good English post-horse would infallibly have born off the prize. We were refreshed at the Governor's, in our return, with tea, coffee, etc., and from thence went home to sleep, and to adorn ourselves for the ball.

Now do not suspect me of minding such a thing, for I only mention it for its singularity —for to me it was beyond measure singular, that the handsome insensible I had honoured so abundantly, in the face of all my admirers, should not have the politeness to ask the favour of my hand for the evening—insomuch that I resolved, if he attempted it on my appearing in the ball-room, I would refuse him.

Note, Arabella, if you take it in your head to wish to know the dresses of the company, either male or female, I shall refer you to the fashions in England in their highest and most expensive state of ornament and decoration. For, except, in the article of mourning, (which is chiefly the beautiful cassemires, which are the produce and manufactures of the East) there is little difference between the appearance of a fine lady at Bengal, and a fine lady in London—for fine ladies in London have found out the elegance of enwrapping themselves in shawls ; and those treasures of the mine, and of the ocean, diamonds and pearls, are well known in England, though not in such profusion ; for those displayed at the ball-room would, moderately speaking, have purchased half a dozen principalities.

I can, however, at length justify the propriety of Doyly's behaviour (the name of my new acquaintenance) from finding he knew, though I did not, the etiquette of balls at

Calcutta ; for you must know the Eastern
ladies, in order to preserve the peace and good
order of society, as well as to promote the
felicity of the evening, never dance above
two country dances with one and the same
gentleman—accordingly, you will perceive had
Doyly taken advantage of my want of information, the trees of destruction would,
the ensuing. morn, have been witness to the
bloodshed, of which I should have been the
innocent, he the guilty cause.

The youth, however, kept close to my
father the whole evening, (on which account, I
doubt not, it was that I was taken in a soft
moment) when, with a diffidence and respect
the Eastern air will soon cure him of, he besought the honour of going down *one* dance
with me——though on recollection, he did
not arrive at this high point of courage, until
my father had sanctioned his presumption by
one of his speaking smiles. He approached
me, bowed, and bowed again—when, (could
you have supposed it ?) my hand, without the
concurrence of my heart, was delivered up to
him, and he had conducted me to my seat,
before I was sensible of my breach of resolution respecting him.

In short, my sweet friend, if nabobism was not the stumbling-block of my ambition, and flattery here the daily incense of the sex, there is no saying what might happen ; for Doyly's flattery is of a most insinuating kind—his eyes are full of expression, and the language of good sense flows from his lips ;—but, I have a vow, that stares my conscience in the face, on the bare mention of Doyly's winning talents—and it is well I have : for, instead of the ceremony of appointing a distant day, and all the dangling visits paid in consequence thereof, you are liable, at Calcutta, to be plundered of your consent any evening of your life ; and, without time to collect yourself, much less to retract—by the Padra's being one of the Company, may be induced to give him a claim to twenty gold mohrs, before he takes his leave ; and so, my good Arabella, being married in haste, be left to repent at leisure.

The only remedy for which evil is, that, instead of the mortification so often experienced in England, on the matrimonial disenchantment, you have innumerable methods of filling up your time agreeably, and are not less beloved by the world, for loving your husband no longer.

After what I have already written of magnificent entertainments, it must be unnecessary to mention, that our supper and sideboard were magnificent.

The ball-room, at the Court-house, is spacious, and finely illuminated—the attendance princely—and the ladies angels.

> Amongst the rest young Edwin bow'd,
> But never talk'd of love :

of which picture, Edmund Doyly is the original, as you will discover in the course of my epistles.

Watson's Works, a place for building bugeros and small sloops, (the road to which lies across the esplanade, to the river, in an oblique direction) is some miles from Calcutta —and to Watson's Works, in order to see the launching of a large bugero, built on a new construction, we repaired yesterday, after taking our tea ; and do but conceive the *éclat* of half a dozen, or more, of these Eastern barges, all freighted with elegant parties, gliding down the stream together, the oars beating time to the notes of the clarinets and oboes.

Music has charms, says the poet, to sooth a savage breast—what power must it then

have over a humanified one, and especially
in an elegant bugero !—the heavens the most
glorious canopy I ever beheld, and the surface of the water crystalline beyond all imagination—the zephyrs !—but I will trust myself with no further description of it, for there
is fascination in the recollection of the scene
—nor have you any thing in England to help
you to the faintest idea of it.

Doyly must, moreover, be brought into the
foreground—his person is so pastoral, and
his sensibility so oriental—had he the Mogul's
diadem, he would place it, I am confident,
upon my head, and, though entitled to all the
privileges of a Mussulman, live for me alone.

But, poor youth ! he has, it seems, his
fortune to make ; and most precarious, of
course, are his prospects of advancement ;
the arrow of disease can impede the accomplishment of the best-conceived designs, ar-
rest the arm of skill, and bring on almost
instantaneous dissolution. I enter, Arabella, into all his delicacies—I feel the fetters
with which he is bound, and am sorry
my father is so encouraging to him, lest a
hope should receive birth therefrom—only
to expire.

The Works are admirable, and the launch gave universal satisfaction—and so profusely were we entertained on the occasion with loll shrub, and every desirable article, that we returned applauding the spirit and politeness of our entertainer.

An accident, however, took place, which will render water parties ineligible to me in future. The beauty of the evening drew all the company upon deck—and a gentlemen in the next bugero to ours, having drank too freely, was noisy and troublesome in his compliments, and so abundantly did he warm with his subject, that, regardless of all danger, he advanced to the unrailed part, and insisted upon the honour of kissing my fair hand. I was not inclined to comply ; for though the rowers are dexterous, I could not help apprehending it would bring the bugeros too close together for our perfect safety :—the company were, however, of a different opinion ; and, ashamed to persist in fears that were peculiar to myself, I leaned forward, supported by poor Doyly, to gratify him—when, to the equal surprise and offence of the whole party, he attempted to salute me. Fired at this boldness, Doyly repulsed him with indignation

and in the same instant was pulled over-
board—and your valiant friend most opportunely fainted away.

He fell not, however, unrevenged—for the
Bacchanalian, a man of large fortune, had
his arm somehow entangled, so that they went
souse together, and were both fished up by
the dexterous Gentoos, (the water being,
as it were, from their diurnal immersions,
their natural element) before I was restored
to life.

I looked anxiously around me, and, from my
then feelings should certainly have relapsed,
if I had not beheld my half-drowned
champion at a distance. The company, as
soon as it appeared no real harm had been
done, very sensibly interposed, and a general
reconciliation succeeded.

Mr. Doyly having changed his dress, joined
us at supper. " I think, Sophia, " said my
father, when he entered the saloon, " I have
not heard you thank this knight for his stroke
of Quixotism in your defence—he was near
paying very dear for it. What reward, my
young friend, shall we bestow upon you ?"

"The honour," replied the gallant Doyly,
"of kissing the hand I preserved from outrage."

I could not forbear telling him, so unusual
was his vivacity on this honour being granted
him, that he appeared much benefitted by his
plunge into the holy river—the waters of the
Ganges being affirmed by the Gentoos to possess, as I have already mentioned, wonderful
virtues.

I expect horrible visions, in consequence of
an incident that has however gone off with
astonishing happiness to all parties—for let
me not attempt to sleep, until I inform you,
that at one o'clock a chit-bearer arrived post
with a letter to Doyly consisting only of these
words :—" If the enclosed is accepted, I shall
then, and then only, have the courage to behold Miss and Mr. Goldsborne again." And
the peace-offering, Arabella, was no less than
an appointment to a private secretaryship,
he had instantly obtained him ; an introduction of all others, the most promising for making a fortune. And may every promise it is
fraught with be fulfilled, though I should
never live to know it!

You may be sure this handsome action met
with due commendation—and Mr. Hartly
said, that if Mrs. D—would permit him to
choose for her, Mr. M. should be the man:

for, as an antidote to intoxication, he must observe, that when he was sober, his heart was liberal, and his manners pleasing. I felt for Mrs. D—; but I might have spared my feelings—she received Mr. Hartly's speech with great good-humour, as a friendly jest— and begged he would give her leave to choose for herself. Doyly is much pleased with this lady; and the fact is, she wins unspeakably on the approbation of us all—and, in every thing but one, I sincerely wish her merit may be rewarded.

LETTER XXI.

Mrs. D—— has new merit in my sight: our phaetons drew up-close to each other on the race-ground, and we had chatted together for a few minutes, when a young fellow, superbly mounted, saluted her with his hat, and asked where he should find her son—she direct-ed him to a distant spot, where I perceived a youth with a plain person, but apparently well satisfied with himself, that put a period to all my nonsensical apprehensions, for he could not be much more than fifteen : an age so unsuitable to mine, as to be alone sufficient security against my father's forming the design I had suspected.

"Is that gentleman your son, " said I, " Madam ? " with an emotion that marked, I am afraid, a rather uncivil surprise. " It is Mr. D——'s son, " replied she, " and as such I acknowledge him—for though his father, on some trifling offence, forgot he was his child, by the fortune he left me, I shall always conceive myself bound to provide for him. " —Perceiving I was about to compliment her upon so generous a way of thinking, she added, " there are duties, my dear young lady, I need not inform you, which it is a reproach to us not to comply with, though no positive institution. I am only the agent of Providence in this business—and should ill deserve the blessings I enjoy (she sighed, Arabella, as if some blessing, nevertheless, was unattained) if I forgot his orphan claims to my protection. "

If this is not greatness of soul, it is something vastly like it, according to my ideas. What claims could this child have to Mrs.

D——'s favour—when his father was the enemy of her peace, and the tyrant of her existence ? It is a sweet feature in her character and shall be revered by me.

Doyly's eyes sparkled with approbation, whilst she uttered the words I have written for your perusal ; and I shall only observe upon the occasion, the different conduct of the world, in different instances—for, had Mrs. D——acted as thousands would have done, towards this miserable-looking boy, the story of her unkindness would have been in every one's mouth—and they would have doubled her fortune in their report, for the pleasure of doubling her guilt. But when her liberality of mind has so honourably displayed itself, even at Calcutta no one was found forward, on the mention of her name, to give her such well-earned praise.

The gentlemen pronounced this day's sport much superior to yesterday's ; but I cannot say I discovered any such thing : however, Arabella, I discovered what gave me great concern, that with the amusement of the turf, the spirit of betting has been imported at Bengal, and the madness is, who shall be first undone.

We passed the night a second time at the Court-house ; but the ball was a compliment of the governor's and well conducted :—and thus our races ended.

The next amusement is the theatre—which would have opened sooner, but from some necessary repairs in the scenery, which were not known to be wanting, until it was too late to accomplish them in the desired time.

My Bramin has been here this morning, and shakes his head at the gay life I lead ; —and, to own the truth to you, Arabella, I am not quite clear, but I have at this moment the seeds of some alarming disease about me : —may you never experience the misery of unstrung nerves ! or your charming spirits become the victim of burning suns, or baneful dews ! My heart dies within me, from the apprehension of what my dear father will suffer, if the mementoes of my mortality, which now hang about me, should increase. Shattered constitutions, expiring friends, last adieus, and melancholy regrets, I cannot tell wherefore, wholly occupy my thoughts —— it may be only fatigue ; or, perhaps, this letter will contain the ultimate levities of my pen. Be assured, however, I shall depart, if my hour

is now come, in the true faith of an European
—the faith confirmed by all around me
—that there is no climate more salubrious than
Britain—no people more blessed—no days
more pleasureable, or nights more tranquil,
than her temperate air bestows. Farewell,
my Arabella! Rapid is the progress of disease in India. I now have just sufficient re-
maining strength to bid you farewell—and
it is not improbable, that by this hour to-
morrow morning I may be in eternity.

Farewell !

————

I MUST write on while I have the power.—
Mrs. Hartly, as is her never-failing kind custom, opened my door to wish me a good-
night. I exerted myself to the utmost, that
the repose of her and her family might not be
interrupted—it will be time enough in the
morning, to make my friends wretched.

Friendly attachments, Arabella, are great
obstacles to piety ; the passage to eternity is,
I grant you, an awful one ; but the thoughts,
I am convinced, linger on temporal ground,
much more from the ties of affection, than the
dread of our future condition. Those whose

lives have been upright, and who have, in repeated instances, been the care of Providence,
dare not doubt of blessedness hereafter ; and
those who have a just sense of the efficacy of
repentance, will have confidence therein, and,
of course, due resignation.

My father, how will he learn to survive me ?
O could I recall my error in one respect, a
most intolerable weight would be taken off
my heart.   Doyly I can point out a comforter
for, and a successor in his tenderness ; a sister
of Mrs. Hartly's, who with, twenty times my
mental merit, is every way my superior in person also ; but I am well aware it will be some-
time before the young man will behold her
with my eyes. My father, my dearest father !
(wicked creature as I have been) who shall
comfort him ?——I grow worse and worse, and
must, I fear, submit to medical regulation.

LETTER XXII.

How fortunate it is for us both, that the
East-India packets arrive not every day ; for
my last letter would have wounded your mind

without any benefit to me.—But I will tell you all that has happened, in my usual narrative manner.

Doyly, I am told, has behaved himself very well during my illness, which, Arabella, was short, but most severe, and has left me so totally emaciated, that this is the first time, for three weeks, that I have been able to resume my pen. He waited whole hours in an anti-chamber, for the purpose of enabling himself to worry my physicians with enquiries how I went on ; which is considered as a high compliment to the patient : and passed his nights in supporting my father. Thank Heaven, I am restored to their wishes, and that Hartly House is delivered from an absolute nuisance of friendly salams, on my account.

My dear Mrs. D.——, (for dear I shall evermore hold her) from a knowledge of Mrs. Hartly's condition, which rendered her unfit for so fatiguing a task, was my regulating nurse. "O fly, Madam," said I to her, when she first presented herself, "fly ; this is assuredly the chamber of death ! "

"I would not knowingly rush upon destruction, " said she, "or hazard my life in a

common cause—but I love you better than a
life of dishonour, which mine would be, if I
forsook my friend in her hour of need :—commit yourself, therefore, as an obligation I
will ever acknowledge, to my care and kindness, and know this is not the first service
of friendship I have successfully engaged
in. Is it not a double life I am anxious
to preserve ?"

"O Madam," cried I, "are we alone ?"
—"We are," replied Mrs. D——. " Then, if
you can divest yourself of apprehensions
from my breath, kneel by me, and compose
my mind by one solemn promise. " " I
kneel, Miss Goldsborne, " said she, " in the
presence of him, I trust, who will preserve you,
and pledge myself to perform whatever you
ask of me, if in my power. "

" My father, Madam, if he survives me,
will you be the sustaining friend of my father ?
—O dearest Madam, I deserve your hate—
your severest displeasure, instead of the affection you bear me ;—for I have dreaded an
event as an evil, that will alone enable me
to die in peace. Wedded to my mother's
memory, his heart is for ever in her coffin, and
in this state has he been left hours, by the

girl, whose felicity was his sole object, to tender melancholy and unavailing lamentation.

What dire enemy of his peace and mine,
suggested the idea to me, that it was merito-
rious in him to be miserable, and filial virtue
in me to rejoice in his misery!" "You must
not agitate yourself in this manner," said
the amiable Mrs. D—— : "nor shall you be
dissembled with on this occasion ;—doubt
not my good-will to relieve your father's mind ;
for, perhaps, that good-will has great share
in my present conduct. Perhaps, Sophia,
all amiable as you are, you would never
have been dear to my heart, had you not
been Mr. Goldsborne's child. Be composed,
therefore, and rest assured, that Providence
will not forsake so worthy a man—he will
be consoled though both you and I were
no more."

"Let me have pen and ink," said I eagerly,
"before my reason is impaired—I will write
but three words, and you shall then do as you
please by me " : a pen and ink was brought
me by a poor Gentoo girl I had been kind to,
who weeping, took Mrs. D——'s place at my
bedside, to give me her best assistance.
wrote as follows :

" Pardon, dear Sir, pardon your child, who, with the prospect of danger before her, is most solicitous for your welfare. You are alone in the world and who shall administer consolation to you when I am no more ?   The blessed spirit of my mother (if the dead are conscious of the actions of the living) is inter-ested in the cause I have at heart :—prove your resignation to heaven, by withdrawing your affections from the ashes of her you have so long survived, and make atonement for the worst sin of my life (wishing an union between you and the only woman on earth capable of soothing your sorrows, might never take place) : and reconcile me, dearest Sir, to myself, by promising me you will solicit her accept-ance of you ;—and be, in my last moment, what I have ever found you, the kindest of fathers to Sophia Goldsborne.''

" Take this,'' said I, to the poor Gentoo girl " take it instantly to my father, and tell him I shall not sleep, until I receive his answer.''

She flew back, with these words, hastily inscribed with a pencil :

" Sleep, my beloved child, thy afflicted father conjures thee to sleep in peace :—he

will observe your request, he will religiously
observe it, as he would a voice from Heaven.
But if you wish him happiness, endeavour to
live ; for his happiness most essentially depends
upon the life of his Sophia—who, living or
dead, shall regulate his future conduct by her
wishes.''

Mrs. D—— was a silent spectator of this
scene, and appeared alone anxious for my
composure :—she gave me my medicines with
her own hand ; and for eight and forty hours
my condition was deemed hopeless. A crisis
then took place—and I will exhaust my
strength no more on this occasion, for have I
not told you I am restored ?

Mrs. Hartly and Doyly have oppressed Mrs.
D——with thanks—my father has alone thank-
ed her, in the happiness he displays on my recovery. I feel for her a daughter's tenderness, a daughter's gratitude, and look forward with rapture to the period, that will give
me the name also—for, Arabella, if preserving
my life (which, under Providence, she has
done) at the hazard of her own, is not a
maternal act, I know not what deserves that
name ;—and I will love her, dearly love her,
for her mental resemblance of her.

————whose worth and charms
Must never more return.

I cannot write longer at present,

So adieu !

S. G.

LETTER XXIII.

But love, the disturber of high and of low.

MY father and Mrs. D—, without speaking a single word to each other on the subject, are certain, from the train into which I have brought things, of their intentions. But Doyly, though he dances round me on my recovery, with ardent delight, breathes not a syllable to me of the state of his affections, or the colour of his wishes :—teizing creature ! I will, Arabella, think (that is, write) no more of him.

You have heard of alligators, (a pretty contrast for the gentle Doyly !) and their depredations, but it seems, unless you throw yourself in their way, in their natural element, the human species have nothing to fear from them, whilst living.

But when the Gentoos, as is one of their pious customs, lay their dead (or, what is more shocking, their dying friends) at low-water mark, that the flowing tide of the sacred Ganges may bury, and purify them from all their sins—the alligators make, together with vultures, and other animals of prey, their feast on them.

The tide, in general, does its office—but not till after the above-described circumstance has taken place—a nuisance, and outrage upon the feelings, I wonder the police do not correct—for besides the appearance, so dreadful to humanity, of mangled limbs and headless trunks, which are daily seen by all who pass that way, impurities must impregnate the air, to augment its native putridity at certain periods, and endanger the lives of the inhabitants of this place.

This disposition of the dead, is a practice confined to a certain number of casts or classes only—for there are other casts, as you may read in the European newspapers, that burn the bodies of their departed friends or relatives, and preserve their ashes with great piety. And of this number are those wives, who, with a degree of heroism, that, if properly directed, would do honour to the female world, make an affectionate and voluntary sacrifice of themselves upon the funeral pile of their departed husbands : —it is true, there have been instances of their shewing reluctance but those instances seldom occur.

No bride ever decked herself out with more alacrity or elegance, than the women about to give this last proof of their conjugal attachment—and they are, no doubt, sanctified to all intents and purposes by the priest's fiat and pass immediately into the presence of Brumma, to receive their reward. This mode of sacrifice, is, however, attended with much expense, or human bonfires would be unending exhibitions; and hence the custom, it is presumable, of burying them in the water ;— and so eager are they to obtain this sacred purification, for those who are past recovery (and, by the way, their superstition forbids their trying the means, in many instances, for their recovery, under the idea of opposing the will of Providence) that they are conveyed with all imaginable piety, and often with their own consent, to the banks of the river, and fitted, by its rising waves, for their translation from earth to heaven.

You have also read of the barbarous exhibition of men, suspended from heights, by
hooks run through the fleshy part of their
shoulders, and stuck on machines barbed
with spikes :—these acts are acts of choice,
in order to restore a poor excommunicated
wretch to the privileges of his cast, or class
—for, on flagrant misbehaviour, they are ex-
cluded, such as eating forbidden things, or
other similar breaches of their religious duties.
And those who survive this display of what
they will do and suffer to atone for their faults
are reinstated in all their forfeited claims,
and their sins are not only forgiven, but forgotten for ever.

I asked my Bramin, on his making me his
congratulation on my recovery, to tell me
what transmigrations (according to the best
of his opinion) would have been my fate, if I
had died, as was expected, in my illness.—
He smiled—blushed I think—and gave me
to understand, that I should never have lost
the power of pleasing, because I have not ex-
ercised that power unworthily in my human
shape. "I suppose then," said I, "I may
conclude, from your complaisance, that I
should have figured away as a cockatoo, or

sung myself into somebody's good graces in
the form of a minho—or perhaps have been
honoured with the person (if I may so call it)
of a Bramine kite.'' He shook his head and
made me believe it very probable, that, as I
had so long been worshipped as a lady, I might
be favoured with divine honours, when I com-
menced one of the feathered race. I am
amused by these little sallies—for well does my
Bramin know, I respect his religious tenets,
though I do not subscribe to them ; and can
never think myself entitled to laugh at any
faith that is seriously adopted, and piously
adhered to.

I, in conclusion, however, told him that,
unless I lost my consciousness with my form,
I should be happy to know myself under his
protection—for I really think so highly of
you, said I, that you are deemed by me one
of the kindest of the kind people to which you
belong. He promised me to observe every
lovely creature, (that was his word) if he survived me, in order to accomplish my wish, and
render himself happy by being useful to me.

Doyly absented himslf suddenly this morning—the dinner and tea have passed away,
and no Mr. Doyly—it is very well—but if he

supposes these unaccounted—for withdrawings
are the way to try my heart, he will soon discover he is mistaken.

I find, to speak the truth, no principles so
steady, or manners so uniform, in all India, as
Mrs.D——'s. She has subdued pride, vanity,
and affectation, or she could not be the woman
she is. And, from the happy effects of my
indisposition, I shall ever rejoice in the recollection of it ; for it was the only means on
earth of opening my eyes to my duty, or on
teaching my heart to perform it.

Doyly, with a face of despair, presented himself at supper. And was rallied, I thought
(notwithstanding all my private wrath) un-
opportunely upon his having been an absentee
contrary to his usual custom. His reply died
on his lips, and I did not dare to meet his eyes
from misgivings of which I could not divine
the cause.

What, Arabella, can have befallen him?—
Has some nabobess made overtures to him,
he is compelled from pre-engagement to decline ? Can he be sentenced to forego the
height of heaven, and toil out his existence
in the diamond mines ? Has he blighted his
little rising prospects at the gaming table, that

bane of prosperity to thousands ? O Doyly—
softly let me speak it—could my fortune
repair the breaches in your's, how immediately, if I was mistress of it, should peace be
restored to your breast ! And fatal experience, your natural good nature and good
sense, would secure you in future from falling. In vain did I seek to read the cause of his
sorrows in both his and my father's countenance ; I am retired to my chamber, agitated
by conjectures. Surely, common friendship
might have induced them to deliver me from
the pangs of suspence and the creations of a
disturbed imagination. Mrs. Hartly taps at
my door—she will relieve me from doubts that
torture me, and fears that threaten I know
not what.

The only misfortune I was unsuspicious of
has befallen me. Doyly sails for Europe to-
morrow, with some important dispatches,
which, from the nature of his new appointment, are entrusted to his care.

Alas, Arabella, who shall hereafter venture
to say an event is prosperous ! when that
most apparently so thus proves, in the person
of poor Doyly, the cause of his greatest mortification. The honour, or the danger, of his

voyage, which shall I teach my mind to dwell upon ? I can anticipate, though I cannot follow, your advice. But what says Shakespear, that great master of human nature ?

Let no one judge of love but those who feel it.

Beware then, my dear girl ! how you dictate decisely in a case, that never was, and perhaps never can be your own.

What medicine can soften the bosom's keen smart,
What Lethe can banish the pain?

Good night, I will no longer expose myself.

———

He breakfasted with us, and my father desired Mrs. Hartly to tell me to bid him adieu, on his embarkation for England. But what adieu can I bid the poor fellow, that will not betray my tenderness for him ? His looks, during the whole period we were together, spoke a language my heart too well understood. Youth of my best approbation ! companion of my pleasantest hours ! whose congenial taste and sentiment has afforded me so much delight ! worthy young man ! farewell ! for ever farewell ! Tell my Arabella all my imputed consequence—paint your own partial estimate of my little merits in their strongest colourings—tell her I possess wealth, fame, admiration—every thing that is desirable, but happiness, and that I alone labour to support existence, for the repose of my father. This was, however, my mental soliloquy, not my address. I shall alarm you, Arabella, by this avowal of my regret, but censure me not, even in your most private thoughts. A friend of either sex, at Calcutta, that is a native of England, and of English education, who can be grave without solemnity, and gay without levity, is a treasure beyond all Golconda can bestow. I will, however, shake off this ill-timed softness and learn to submit myself with a good grace to all the changes and chances of my destiny ; but we can bear our wants much better than our losses, which is a cutting, because an applicable remark on my own situation. Our last hour, however, is not yet come, for he will drink tea with us.

He is gone, Arabella ; and silence was the only language of adieu between us. He eat not, he drank not, he sighed not, but suddenly looking on his watch, and finding he must depart, he kissed both Mrs. Hartly's hands, touched one of mine, barely touched it, with

his lips, and left us—never more, perhaps,
to return !

The good-natured Mrs. Hartly's eyes were
suffused by tears. " There is not, " said she,
"his equal, for his age, in all the East. He
has all the promise about him of being a great
man ; but for my part, well as I wish him, I
could not have prevailed upon myself to ad-
vise him, as your father did, to cross the ocean
and deprive us of his agreeable society."

Every thing but this I supported with fortitude, but the mention of my father's name,
as the author of my distress ; there was no
concealing my feelings ! "And did my father,
Madam, " I stopped, sensible of my error,
Mrs. Hartly, however, as perfectly understood
me, as if I had wrote a volume upon the occasion—and said every soothing, every possible word, that benevolence and friendship
could suggest—and led me to my apartment.
My best prayers, Arabella, will attend him,
but I will mention him no more.

Your's,
S. G.

LETTER XXIV.

My Bramin—how sweet is religion, as described by him !—the love of the Deity, and the love of our fellow-creatures, its fundamentals—and peace and charity the superstructure.

For love, this young priest affirms, refines the sentiment, softens the sensibility, expands our natural virtues, extinguishes every idea of jealously or competitorship, and unites all created beings in one great chain of affection and friendship.

"So far," replied I, "so far, my good Sir, for the happy side of the prospect ;—but what cure have you for the wounds your sensibility must receive by the dissolution of the tenderest ties of friendship, the survival of your dearest connections ?"

"We resolve every event," said the amiable Bramin, "into the divine appointment, and dare not repine."

"This is very delightful doctrine in theory, Sir," returned I. "And salutary in practice, Madam," replied he, "as the man before you is a living testimony ;—for that he was born a Bramin, he submits to, as the will of Heaven—and that you are the loveliest of women, he acknowledges with pious resignation.''

I was astonished—Mrs. Hartly was silent —and the Bramin retired, with more emotion than quite accorded with his corrected temper, as if he felt he had said too much.

Wretch that I am, Arabella ! this confession which I shall ever remember with pain, did I, in the idle gaiety of my heart, ardently aspire after. O, how I lament, that young men and women (with few exceptions, I am afraid) cannot form a friendship of the tranquil and liberal kind, a friendship that ends not in an exclusion of all other attachments, I mean as to precedents ! A life of voluntary celibacy, an unsocial state, which nature revolts at, is the life of a Bramin—for the joys of conversation surpass all other joys, they are the peculiar blessing of the human race. And you find, Arabella, the mental claims are the same in all —for, that I am a conversible being, is the attraction with this Gentoo devotee. I therefore at length see, and subscribe to, the wisdom of confining their amusements to their pagodas, and their public shews ; for they have hearts made for society, and, having once tasted the pleasures social intercourse gives, must pass their days in secretly condemning what they openly profess to approve, the misconceived tenets of Brumma—for I am clear, the wonderful and enchanting gift of speech was not bestowed upon us to be sons and daughters of solitude.

Doyly's departure has only been a prelude to the loss of our Governor, and every creature is plunged into disconsolation Not a bugero will be unoccupied—it is the last proof of their heartfelt respect they can shew him ; and you may judge of the preparation, when I tell you, it is an absolute voyage they have resolved upon, to do him honour.

The Company it is affirmed by those who appear well informed, will, by this event, be deprived of a faithful and able servant ; the poor, of a compassionate and generous friend ; the genteel circles, of their best ornament ; and Hartly House of a revered guest.

He has three times, it seems, stood forth, in his late public station, the worthy character I found him—and his plans of government have procured him the repeated thanks and plaudits of the Company.—But,

Envy will merit, as its shade, pursue.

A more uniform good man, or so competent
a judge of the advantages of the people, he
will not leave behind him ; nor possibly can a
successor be transmitted, of equal information and abilities. For, Arabella, he has made
himself master of the Persian language, that
key to the knowledge of all that ought to
constitute the British conduct in India, or
can truly advance the British interest. But
I am getting upon political ground ; and
will only add, as the friends of this gentleman observe, that, as the sun is often ob-
scured, without lessening its brightness, so
the clouds, which have so unaccountably
gathered around his fame, *may* I say, (*will*
they say) be one day universally and ultimately dispelled.

The whole place is engaged in adieus, and
Mrs. H——will be accompanied to England
(for the Governor sails in a different ship) by
a Mrs. M—— who has been presented with
500 gold mohrs (a thousand pounds) in return
for her complaisance in making the voyage
with her. Two black girls and a steward,
are Mrs. H—'s attendants ; and the state
cabin and round-house will be entirely devoted
to her use.

My father wishes me to make one in Mrs. D—'s bugero ; but I think it impossible I can comply with that wish—so recently as poor Doyly has quitted us, and so distressing as all bidding adieu is to the feelings of your

S. G.

LETTER XXV.

IT is over, and we behold our Governor no more. He would have taken leave of his friends at Diamond Point, but they would not hear of such a thing—their bugeros were well stored with provisions, and every requisite, etc., so with pendants flying, and bands of music, to the last man and instrument to be found in Calcutta, they attended him to Sawger, the extremity of the river.

He was, moreover, saluted by nineteen guns from every Indiaman at Bengal, and the general voice, in all quarters, continues to be, they ne'er shall look upon his like again.

They returned not, Arabella, until they beheld the packet and Indiaman sail out of soundings ; in the former of which was the

Governor, and in the latter his wife : and
then slowly, and with solemn music, made
for Diamond Point, where palanquins, to an
incredible number, were in waiting to
convey them to their respective homes.

I passed the period of their absence at Hartly Bungilo—my father not only consenting to
my declining the party, from a hint of Mrs-
Hartly's that the fatigue would be too much
for me, but laying his injunctions upon me, not
to think of going ;—and Mrs. Rider, and the
children, were unremitting their endeavours
to amuse me, and keep up my spirits.

But I found time for meditation, and the
result is, that I shudder at the narrowness and
illiberality of my past conduct. For what but
narrowness and illiberality of heart, could for
a moment have incited me to suppose that
my father's union with an amiable accomplished woman, would weaken his affection
for me, or throw his conjugal faith and tenderness into shade ?

O Arabella, Arabella, admirably does Roche-
foucault distinguish, when he affirms, "that
there is much more of self-love, than love for
the object, in jealousy ; ''—for, if we love
truly (I am now convinced) in the character

of either husband, wife, child, or friend, the
happiness of those we love will infallibly be
the first rate consideration with us ;—and
that I was not aware of the benefits that must
accrue from having an assisting and relieving
partner in the business of promoting my
father's tranquility, is a crime of my nature
I will not easily pardon.

I intreat you will be very particular in trans-
mitting me all that passes in your interview
with poor Doyly : this request originates solely from common good wishes towards him—
for would it not be an impeachment of the
friendship I bear his *friends*, to be unmindful
of his fate ?—not that I bar your conclusions,
be they what they may, so you only do me
the justice to believe I am,

Your's, most affectionately,

S. G.

LETTER XXVI.

HENCEFORTH, Arabella, you are to consider
me in a new point of view. Ashamed of the

manners of modern Christianity, (amongst
the professors of which acts of devotion are
subjects of ridicule, and charity, in all its
amiable branches, a polite jest) I am become
a convert to the Gentoo faith, and have my
Bramin to instruct me *per diem*.

What a sweet picture would the pen of
Sterne have drawn of this young man's person!
But such is the European narrowness of sentiment, that if I was to attempt to do it, you
would instantly conclude,

I love the precepts for the teacher's sake.

But love, I can assure you, is not so spontaneous an effect (in general) of a friendship
between the sexes in India as in England;
the object of admiration being mental charms,
which bid defiance to decay. .

The Mahometans have their public processions as well as the Gentoos; but the colour of
their minds, so unlike that amiable people, is
displayed therein—for the Gentoos dance,
sing, and pay their enraptured homage to
their idols with benevolent aspects—whereas
the custom of the sons of Omar is to exhibit
sham-fights, as they are called, though often
productive of very fatal and barbarous

consequences—insomuch that, on my first knowledge of the light and darkness these religious shews are to each other, I felt myself in danger of becoming a *Braminate*, though all the wealth of Indostan could not bribe me to become a Mahometan.

And striking, indeed, are the opposite tenets of these opposite people—for the Gentoos, with a liberality of temper for which I shall ever honour them, bestow souls without number, and existence without end, on both sexes; —the proud Mussulmen make a monopoly of immortality in their own persons—for which piece of unauthorized daring, I am unable to restrain my indignation towards them, nor would honour even the nabob himself with an exception, but that I have hopes of his apostacy—for, Arabella, whenever the time shall arrive when either your charms or mine are destined to convince him he has a heart to fall a victim thereto, he will not, he cannot, persist in refusing us a soul also. Then his wealth pleads so powerfully for him, and his high-sounding title, and his magnificence altogether, that one has very little to say in his disfavour. If you have made the observation that the wicked tyrant Surajah

Dowla, the destroyer of the English at Calcutta, is styled a Soubah, you may perhaps
wish to understand the difference between a
Soubah and a Nabob. The Moors, or Mahometan princes, are said to have introduced
the division of India into provinces, or, as they
are called in their language, soubahs; which
provinces, being of such immense extent as to
form whole empires, were sub-divided into
nabobships, every nabob of course being immediately accountable to his soubah for his
conduct and government. But in process of
time, from internal commotions and irrepressible invasions, both soubahs and nabobs became almost independent of the Mogul himself, or at least held their dominions under
him by the sole tenure of an annual tribute.
The rajahs, or kings, as you will find in the
history of Indostan, are the unconquered
Black Monarchs, who possess the Northern
provinces, and furnish the Mogul emperor, or
any other prince, with troops of their own
complexion, called Rajapoots, from their
royal descent; who fight like the Swiss for pay,
without any curiosity or principle respecting
the cause of contest. But a droll practice of
theirs is, that on beholding their leader slain,

they instantly deem themselves absolved from
every engagement, and, openly laying down
their arms, run out of the field—and this without incurring the slightest impeachment of
their courage.

The great military officers of the Mogul are
called Omrahs, and if they have been generals,
they are called Mirzas. But though the Pa-
gan rajahs and nobility inherit the honours
and estates of their ancestors, there are no
such thing as hereditary honours or estates
amongst the Moors or Mahometans ; but, on
their decease, all their possessions, real and
personal, are seized by the sovereign, as in
Turkey.   And, Arabella, you have heard much
in England of jaghires, which I can inform
you are neither more or less than these lands,
which revert, on the death of a Mahometan
chief, etc., to the emperor ; by whom they are
sometimes bestowed on those who occupy
them, and sometimes are their personal
acquisitions : some of which our countrymen have obtained as *douceurs* on certain
great occasions; their merits on those occasions, however, are not always either obvious or satisfactory to the higher powers
in England.

Politics again !—but I am on the point of being furnished with a far more agreeable sub-ject—for the theatre opens to-morrow, with Love in a Village—it opens, Arabella, when Doyley is absent—when your friend's heart is—and why should not your friend's heart be occupied by soft sentiments ?—for, in a country where so large a number of its inhabi-tants dare to deny her a soul, sure she may amuse herself with feeling she has a heart. O how I at this moment wish myself in England ! I am fascinated, to write so much about such wicked unbelievers.

Adieu,

Your's, etc.,

S. G.

LETTER XXVII.

THE theatre, Arabella, is opened and to-night will be honoured with my presence. The door-keepers are, I am told, Europeans ; for the black people, in an office of that nature, would have no authority with the public.

The doors will be opened at eight o'clock ; but the performance seldom terminates, I am told, till twelve or one in the morning.

Mrs. D——, Mrs. and Mr. Hartly, my father, the country-born lady I have so often mentioned, and Miss Hartly, (mentioned by me only in a melancholy mood, previous to my illness) accompany me ; but alas ! Arabella, I have not the requisites about me, I had promised myself, for participating in this, my nevertheless favourite amusement ; for what says the poet ?

> ——Not of themselves the gay beauties can please.
> We only can taste, when the heart is at ease.

We go in palanquins, and shall make a fine illumination with our flambeaux ; nor can you imagine a sight more extraordinary, than the contrast of the Gentoo complexion with their white dresses, or the advantage I am well aware it is to us Europeans, in general, to have them about us ; for who does not know the alternate and striking effects of black and white ? The artillery officers will also, I suppose, figure away in the boxes, and their uniform is elegant—blue, trimmed with silver— smart fellows, I can assure you ; besides the recommendation of being men of taste and sensibility, as I could, if this was one of my vain moments, give you some undeniable proofs that they are.

Few things are more uncommon (or, let me tell you, more exemplary) than Mrs. D— and my father's behaviour to each other ; she having the good sense not to be *obtrusive* —he the good principle not to be a hypocrite : they meet, without the folly of appoint-ment, wherever they go, and are certain of speaking each other's sentiments in all con-versations. I have observed my father pen-sive, without knowing the cause, until he has looked around and perceived Mrs. D——ab-sent ; when he has mechanically (so natural has been the action to his feelings) en-quired if she was not expected—and twice, Arabella, on hearing she was confined at home with a cold—giving me a look of gentle reproach, he ordered his palanquin, to make her a visit. If I ask his opinion, he refers me to Mrs. D—— ; and on his ap-plying to me for my choice in any instance, I always beg him to consult that lady. " Her eye," I said to him this morning, " my dear Sir,is become my law—my oracle, her tongue."

—"Grateful winning girl," he called me, "child of his tenderest affection;" and, pausing a moment, "in return for your open, your liberal-mindedness, you shall know all that has passed in your father's heart.

"Mrs. Hartly has a thousand perfections; of one fault, my Sophia, you must therefore permit me to accuse her : she did not do justice to Mrs. D——, in her manner of communicating either to me, or you, the approbation with which that lady honoured me ; in consequence of which, the first impression you received of Mrs. D—— was not a favourable one.

"But I was well acquainted with Mrs. D——'s noble disposition, and numberless accomplishments ; and was therefore happy, since I could not offer her my hand, to soften my seeming neglect of her, and ungentlemanly return for her singular kindness, by soliciting her friendship for my Sophia.

"For, Sophia, at that period it was my fixed resolution to end my days in the East. I will not wound you by the mention of my motives ; but my whole soul was in the desire of your establishment in England. Mrs. D——'s fortune enabled her to live under whatever meridian she liked best ; and, from my knowledge of the female mind, I was persuaded no event could be more likely to take place, on her meeting with a little disappointment in India, than that she should make England her place of residence ; and to whose care could I have so satisfactorily intrusted my Sophia as Mrs. D——'s whose generous way of thinking has made her a parent to the son of her cruel husband ?

" I told her my resolution respecting myself, with circumstances that melted her into tears you would have honoured, for your deceased parent was the object of them ; and she assured me she would be all that dear departed one herself could wish to render her, in your service. Your attachment to her, your filial anxiety for me, have produced a most unforeseen alteration in the sentiments of us all. I remain not at Bengal, when she and you determine to quit it ; but, by Mrs. D——'s request, I mention no change of condition to her in India. We meet with pleasure, we part with friendship ; and, in a word, our manner of considering each other here, is an implied prelude to our living together in England ; and this is a victory over my feeling, the view, as I believed, of your approaching dissolution could alone have effected :—but I am now convinced we both acted wrong. Your mother can never indeed be forgot by us, however wisely or piously we may bring ourselves to accept happiness at the hands of Providence, let it assume what shape it may.

Mrs. Hartly broke up our *tete-a-tete*, by telling us we should not be ready for dinner, if I did not make dispatch at my toilet.

I am, therefore, in great haste,

Your's, &c.,
S. G.

LETTER XXVIII.

Miss Hartly and Miss Rolle, the country-born lady I introduced to your knowledge with her hooka before her, are only occasionally our visitants ; for, in order to finish their education in a few particulars, they are, it seems, placed at a boarding-school, the only one in Calcutta, in much esteem with the Europeans.

The stipend, you may be assured, is considerable, but I have not yet qualified myself to announce it. There masters in every polite science attend, and there are public days for the friends of the children to see them dance, in like manner as in England; and at this school both the young ladies are to remain, until proposals may be received for their change of condition. Their fortunes are small (for Calcutta fortunes) twenty-thousand rupees only; but I think there can be little doubt of Miss Hartly's marrying well, from her own great merit, and her brother's good connections.— Had young D. been a better figure, and his mind such as I could wish it, I would have tried my hand, for the first time, at matchmaking. I might have thought, you will perhaps say, of Doyly; but Doyly, I have already told you, is poor, and consequently such a union would ruin them both: besides, Arabella, why should you be so provoking as to suggest him, when you know he is gone to England.

Morn. 4 *o'clock.*

I have been greatly entertained—the company, Arabella, was brilliant ; and a birthnight could alone have eclipsed us.

The house is about the size of the Bath Theatre, and consists, as I was informed on my first arrival, of pit and boxes only : the fisrt, an area in the center ; the second, a range of commodious enclosed, or rather separated, seats round it, from one corner of the stage to the other. No expence has, Arabella, been spared to gratify either the eye or the ear— a very pleasing band of music saluted the present Governor on his entrance—and the pit was crouded with spectators. It is lighted up upon the English plan, with lamps at the bottom of the stage, and girandoles at proper distances, with wax candles, covered with glass shades, as in the verandas, to prevent their extinction ; the windows being Venetian blinds, and the free circulation of air delightfully promoted by their situation.

The character of Young Meadows was very agreeably supported by one of the Company's writers, a young gentleman that visits at Mr. Hartly's, and is in a rising way. Moreover,

if I have any skill in physiognomy, he does
not behold the sister of that house with un-
favourable eyes, and I must mention as much
to Mrs. Hartly. Hawthorn was performed
by an adjutant in the artillery ; Deborah
Woodcock, by poor Doyly's patron, who has
much pleasantry ; Rosetta by a young gentleman in the law department ; Lucinda, by the
son of an East India captain ; and in like manner were the other characters filled up ; and
I do declare upon my word and honour, that
I was as well entertained as if the female parts
had been sustained by females—and again
wish, in the cause of morality, the custom
could be re-established in England. The scenery was beautiful, and the dresses superb.
Here Golconda's wealth in all its genuine lustre astonished the beholder, and a profusion
of ornamental pearls were disposed with good
taste ; in a word, whether it was the poet, or
the performers, or the diamonds, or the air
of enchantment they all together certainly wore,
I know not ; but so pleasing an effect had the
whole upon my mind, that I forgot Doyly,
my native country, my Arabella, and my mother, and, for the only period of my residence
at Bengal, was completely happy.

Several country-born ladies figured away
in the boxes, and by candle-light had absolutely the advantage of the Europeans ; for their
dark complexions and sparkling eyes gave
them the appearance of animation and health
the Europeans had no pretensions to ; and
their persons are genteel, and their dress magnificent. Whereas, on the other hand (speaking for myself at least) paleness and languor
told the country of my birth, and were not to
be concealed or compensated by all that polite
negligence, or accomplished manners, could do.

The pit was full of gentlemen of every denomination, which gentlemen paid their compliments, at convenient pauses, to the ladies ;
who, by the aids of perfumes and verandas, of
fruit and of flattery, went through the fatigue
of the evening with a good grace, and were
conveyed home, as they were conveyed there,
in their palanquins, in very tolerable spirits.

As for myself, my attention was so engaged
by the piece, that my heart several times
asked if it could be possible I was at the
distance of 4,000 miles from the British
metropolis ?

Lionel and Clarissa is to be the next
performance.

The gentlemen to whom we were indebted for our evening's entertainment, were soon at our supper-table ; and the evening would have been concluded with a rational degree of cheerfulness, beyond all one can hope for in large companies, but for a little incident I shall mention :—Doyly's patron was so generous (having dispatched him, poor fellow, across the ocean on an embassy) to declare himself his rival. I was almost sorry the Gentoos had taken so much pains to fish him up on the Bugero disaster, and could alone consider him as the enemy of a youth whose life he had most cruelly a second time endangered—for who knows not the precarious safety of him who rides upon the waves ? This declaration was laughed off ; but having swallowed his compliment of claret, he no less suddenly than forcibly seated himself between Mrs. D—— and me ; and, calling every power to witness that he would have one of us, boisterously kissed Mrs. D—'s cheek. I trembled for my father's feelings ; nor was she, I believe, without her tender alarms. However, with a command of temper that astonished me, so present was she to the occasion, that she told him, on condition he gave

up his chair to Mr. Hartly, she would be glad
to hear how handsomely he could make love
to her the next morning ; and handsomely
she was convinced, (by the abilities he had
displayed in the character he had performed)
he could acquit himself in every instance.
This had the desired effect ; and Mr. Hartly
exchanging seats with him, universal harmony
was restored.   Mr. Hartly, however, whispered
us that he must give him a civil hint such
freedoms were not to be repeated in his house.

How I rejoiced in the circumstance, which,
but a moment before, was no soothing recollection ! for the winds and the waves, in their utmost wrath and violence, could alone rob
Doyly of his existence ; whereas, had he died
in a quarrel, of which I was the cause, could
I have attempted to survive him ?   I would
not be this bold man's wife, was he the
Great Mogul himself.

My opinion was then asked by the gentlemen, my genuine opinion (as being a competent judge, from my acquaintance with the
London theatres) of the Calcutta candidates
for fame on theatrical ground ; and it was with
pleasure I could, and did sincerely assure
them, that I found good sense was sufficient

to make a gentleman a player, though all the professional excellence on earth, without good-breeding and liberal connections, could not make a player a gentleman.

My father and Mrs. Hartly exchanged a look (for I did not perceive their lips move) that was perfectly intelligent to each other, and Mrs. D——left us not, nor is she to leave us until to-morrow evening ; so it is plain my father was not an unmoved spectator of the rough scene. I shall dream, Arabella, of those horrible trees of destruction—and most heartily do I wish myself in England.

Yours,
S. G.

LETTER XXIX.

HALF a word of Doyly, and I have done.— Should he arrive safe, Arabella, and deliver into your hands the *chit* with which I have intrusted him, treat him kindly, for he has a truly valuable heart.

My father was in the breakfast-room before me—not so Mrs. D—— ; for she had slept little, she said, and complained of the headach.

My father's eyes met mine ; he was greatly alarmed—" If we should lose you, Madam, " said he, in a low voice, walking up to her, " how ardently shall I wish my Sophia had never known you. "

" I shall do very well," replied she, smiling, " I hope, notwithstanding the endeavours of all your friendly countenances to terrify me. Bear witness, Mr. Hartly, if I die, I pronounce myself the victim of the dismal faces around me." We all made an aukward attempt to smile, in return to this lively sally ; but Mrs. D——protested it was a vile imitation, and begged us to desist. " However, " said she, " though I am unwilling to prolong so melancholy a scene, (having beheld disease in various forms, and well knowing that the most severe attack must have its commencement) I think I should be unpardonable, not to set my house in some little order. Is there any one in this company so weak, " cried she, looking around her, " as to suppose the idea of making a will a bad omen ? If so, let them be turned out, for they are a disgrace to good sense, and an insult to piety. " We were all silent. "Have you, Mr. Goldsborne, never made your will?" "Yes, Madam," replied my father, "within these last three weeks of my life—and have presumed to appoint you, without either your knowledge or consent, my executrix, in one instance."

"I will be more polite than you then," said she, "and solicit permission to encumber you with the care of a young man, who, if he survives me, will not have a friend on earth to guide him aright. His temper is not without faults," continued she, "but I do hope his heart is in the right place ; and your friendship will awe him into the adoption of your example. Sophia, my gentle Sophia, take your pencil, and, before the lawyer arrives, commit what I shall tell you to paper." I obeyed ; but my hand shook in such a manner I was fearful I could not form a letter. "To Sophia Goldsborne," said she, "I bequeath my firmness of mind, that she may never more be found incapable of assisting a friend in need. But I think I am better ; and so, Miss Sophia, put up your pencil with your trembling hand, and let me be left alone with Mr. Hartly, who is the only person present that does not wear the features of my executioner ;

and yet I am confident he takes as kind an
interest in my health and safety, as the best
of you all."

"Mrs. D——can be insincere," said I,
"which is a sin of the heart ; whereas the offence
I committed against her was the sin of my
constitution."

"I deny it," said she, "your heart was
equally guilty with mine ; for virtues are vices,
when productive of baneful consequences."

My father arose, bowed, and was withdrawing. "Why, Mr. Goldsborne," said Mrs.
D——, "if I was not afraid of your opposing
my last will and testament, I should not have
the least objection to your being present
when the gentleman I have sent for arrives
Do you allow it is lawful for a woman to dispose of her property to her wishes ? or would
you recommend the delicacies and romantic
fancies of her friends for her rule of conduct ?
I have (but do let us all sit quietly down)
a good deal of wealth. Young D——shall
receive from me as much as he can spend with
a good grace. And now, Mr. Goldsborne, I
ask your advice, who shall I leave the remain-
der to ? Relations I never heard of (if such relations are upon the earth). To the patron

of poor Doyly, in return for kindnesses received ? or do you allow it to be reasonable I
should bestow it upon one I love, though that
one should happen to be your own daughter ?
I will lay a thousand pounds you give judgment against my inclination.''

"You do me injustice, Madam,'' replied
my father ; '' may you long live to enjoy
your fortune ! but, should my daughter be
fated to survive you, I hope I can answer for
her being grateful to your memory, for every
mark of your affection you may be pleased
to confer on her.''·

'' You surprise me, '' said Mrs. D——, '' you
most agreeably surprise me.''

'' Then I have done more by you, Madam,
than your utmost generosity to my daughter
will do by me. However, since we have been
led so far upon the subject of wills, I must beg
you will do me the favour to read mine ; ''
and, taking out his pocket-book, he broke
the seals of a small packet, and put it into
her hands.

'' It is very concise,'' said she ; '' but I hope
there is some mention of Mrs. D——, that
will prove to her that her friendship for this
company does not so far outstrip the friendship

entertained for her as she may imagine.''
—Many were the changes of countenance she
exhibited, whilst she perused it. '' You have
made me quite vain,'' said she, '' Sir, by in-
trusting me with the contents of this paper ;
and I am not, then, in danger of becoming
less worthy of your good opinion ? '' I felt
my curiosity interested, but would not shew
it ; and my father returned it into the pocket-
book from whence he had taken it.

The lawyer now arrived, and young D——
came soon after. The business was, however,
soon over ; and Mrs. D——, with great kindness, called to tell me she was not worse, and
waited to introduce her son. I made all possible haste to dress, and hurried into her apartment ; but fancying she looked very ill, all
the vivacity, the lively assurance of her not
being ill, had given birth to in my breast,
forsook me, and I could only say, '' Is this,
Madam, the young gentleman ?''

Mr. D——(for, early days as it is with him,
he assumes that title) made me a very decent
bow ; and, upon the whole, appeared much less
disagreeable in his person, than on my first
view of him ; and I could perceive she was
pleased that I paid him some attention. He

did not, however, stay long with us ; and she
told me, as soon as we were alone, I should
greatly oblige her by saying what I really
thought of a plan she had formed, in her own
mind, for his establishment. " In the first
place, observe, my Sophia, I mean to give him
a good fortune, and, of course, enable him to
chuse a woman less amply provided for, if her
connections and character are recommenda-
tory. Miss Hartly is an agreeable girl ; and,
I think, comes in every respect under my
description. She is too happy, nevertheless,
with all her merit, to be troubled with your
nicety of temper ; and will not disdain to hear
a generous matrimonial proposal from a young
man, though his person may not be the most
unexceptionable in the world. He is not ill-
tempered, though a coxcomb ; and she will
only have to humour his foibles, to do what
she pleases with him. Is my scheme good
or bad ?"

"We do not," said I, " Madam, behold
Miss Hartly with the same eyes. To me, she
is elegant in her person, and lovely in her manners." And, Arabella, as from the abundance of the heart (you know the proverb) we
are apt to speak, I was within a hair's breadth

of telling her my scheme for Doyly; but check-
ing myself, "Madam," said I, "is not the
gentleman very young?" "He is turned of
twenty," said she. (I was amazed; for on
the course. I did not suppose it possible he could
be more than sixteen at the utmost.) "Eighteen
years of which," continued Mrs. D——,
"I have had him under my care, if I may so
express myself, when the fact is that half the
time I scarcely ever beheld him, and he was
not encouraged to bear me much respect.
He is one of those that improve upon acquaintance; and though no genius, does not
want for sense. His coxcombry is his only
great fault; and time and a discreet wife, I
think, will do much towards extinguishing
that folly."

Everybody went to 'Lionel and Clarissa,'
except Mrs. D——, my father, and myself,
who played a short pool at quadrille. It was
not, however, to be concealed, that though
Mrs. D——did her best to make us happy,
she was indisposed, and I prevailed with her
to retire early.

I will only take upon me to answer for myself; but certain it is, I passed the night in
great anxiety and self-condemnation. Had

I not been the illiberal girl I have been, it is most probable we should have avoided the present threatening evil. Let no one hereafter, who would escape self-reproach—escape self-condemnation—fail to improve every possible opportunity of promoting the happiness of their friends; for, ultimately, that conduct will be to promote their own. What was it I feared? That my dear father to love his wife, must cease to love his child? and thence, in the moment I was professing the warmest filial affection for him, prefer a situation for him that must, on any change of condition I might urn my thoughts to, leave him comfortless and companionless! Nay, how could I find the pleasure I did in Mr. Doyly's conversation, without remembering how many melancholy hours the conversation of such a woman as Mrs. D—— could preserve my father from experiencing?

I, to the disobedience of every injunction I had received, and the breach of every promise I had made, was in Mrs. D——'s chamber at seven o'clock, and had the grief to find her unable to sit up; he confessed to me, that Mr. Emson (Doyly's patron) had frightened

her; and imputed her indisposition solely
to that cause. "But this is a piece of information," said she, "we must not give
your father. The quarrels of men are so
alarming, that whoever wishes to prevent
mischief must be cautious how they breathe
inflammatory complaint before the sex, lest
some idle or fatal point of honour should
make them conceive themselves bound to re-
sent, or even to remonstrate with the offending party."

I went down to breakfast with the most
cheerful look I could assume ; and, as we were
only a family set this morning, by way of
amusing my friends, I mentioned Mrs. D——'s
wishes respecting Miss Hartly ; and contrary
to my expectations, found her perfectly right.
Mr. Hartly said, "The offer was equal to
whatever his sister had a right to expect ; and
that the kind intentions of such a mother as
Mrs. D——were full security for the felicity
and provision of the woman she was so generous as to make the object of her choice, and
honour with her friendship and protection."
This had the desired effect, and filled up the
breakfast hour ; but, on my acknowledging
that Mrs. D——did not think of dining with

them, a cloud of discontent hung on every
brow. Mr. Hartly was so good as not to
leave my father ; and I, with a heavy heart,
revisited Mrs. D——. In the evening, however, her physician assured us she was not in
the smallest danger ; and so we were all convinced, and, therefore, very freely forgave
him the *prudent* attention it was evident he
meant to pay to his own interest ; nor did he
pronounce his visits unnecessary, until he
had pocketed two hundred gold mohrs.
Who then shall complain, but the sons of
Esculapius, in England, understand a little
manœuvring ; or, when occasion fairly
presents itself, contrive to reimburse some
of the great expence of time and fortune,
which is inevitable, before they can obtain their diploma ? I protest it would be
for the good of society at large, in Britain,
if some characters, I could mention, were to
smart for one twelve months under the ex-
actions from which there is no defence in
India for the man or woman of wealth,
except flying the country ; nor do I conceive, if Mrs. D——would tell the truth, that
the law and medicine, she has so recently
tood in need of, has cost her less than five

hundred pounds sterling in so short a period
as four days.

Mrs. D—— is gone home—and it is re-
ported, that Mr. Emson sails next month for
Europe—two circumstances that have had
so agreeable an operation on our feelings,
that we go to the play to-morrow evening
(the Conscious Lovers) ; and I shall the next
morning resume my custom of telling you all
I learn of this country and its inhabitants.
For, so numerous are the people of England
connected with the East, that I am well satisfied I shall enable you to figure away, to the
delight of three-fifths of the company into
which you will circulate, in consequence of
my equally *entertaining* and *intelligent* correspondence. Nor is there any impropriety
or indelicacy, Arabella, in saying a handsome thing of ourselves, when we are so
situated, (which, at the present writing, is
the case with me) that it must otherwise
be *unknown*.

Congratulate us, I charge you, on our cause
for rejoicing respecting Mrs. D—— ; and,
if Doyly is with you, when this letter arrives,
communicate the contents, and he will truly
rejoice also ; for he has the most sincere and

abundant good-will for her of any one I am acquainted with, my father excepted.

I am yours, etc., etc.,

S G.

———

LETTER XXX.

THE natives of Bengal have no dirty customs like the Europeans. For example, if a snuff-taker is mentioned, you know he, or she, is an European, insomuch that, partial as I am to my native country, I must wish that it would take a lesson from hence, and reprobate several propensities I could name, that are altogether incompatible with the virtue of cleanliness. Your own observation will suggest the points of indecorum, not to say, indecency, which I allude to.

I was startled, within this half hour, by the discharge of guns ; for, though the affair of the Black Hole is but little remembered at this distant period at Calcutta, I myself am unable to forget it. Accordingly, with emotions I will not stop to describe, I sent to enquire the cause of the firing at the Fort, etc., etc.

The funeral of one of the Company's officers was the answer I received ; and the minute guns were continued for some time, with a solemn effect on my feelings ; nor could I suppress a wish to see the procession—but that was negatived by all my friends ; and yet, Arabella, to me, this kind prohibition heightened the concern I took in the affair. Death again ! It is a subject that insensibly forces itself upon my notice, and tinges my most brilliant efforts at agreeable description with a gloom, I fear, you must find contagious.

The tide of the Ganges (for I will change my subject) for three successive months flows one way ; so that though ships can at all seasons (as far as that article is accommodating) leave Calcutta, no ship, on any extremity whatever, for three months can effect its navigation thereto ; a circumstance that accounts for what you may often hear mentioned, of Indiamen losing their passage to this coast, and being obliged to defer it until the sacred river becomes propitious.

I own I was much disappointed by my view of the banks of the Ganges, for I expected to have seen them ornamented with every beauty of the vegetable world, the spontaneous product of the soil ; instead of which, its borders are unfavoured by nature, and uncultivated by art ; and alone exhibit a sameness of prospect wholly uninteresting to the beholder.

The immediate shores of Culpee and Cudjelee, where, as I have already mentioned, the Indiamen are stationed (though not so strictly as heretofore, for some of them come up as high as Diamond Point) are visited by both officers and sailors—who, having made a fire, sit fearless around it in the very face of enemies that would chill my blood with horror—for tigers, I am assured, approach so near as to be within a bound or two of the spot they occupy ; though no instance has ever yet occurred, in which the fire has not proved their infallible security. Would one conceive it possible, Arabella, that any of the human species could sit with tranquility amidst the howlings of formidable brutes, prompt to devour ? All the sea forms are observed, on entering the mouth of the Ganges, of hoisting the pendant for pilots and receiving the salutes of the ships previously arrived, in their passage to the Hughley, the name

under which a branch of this celebrated river
runs for above fifty miles and on the most
western part of which the New Fort is erected.

And now I mention the Fort, I recollect I
have not yet told you that the public prison
is within its walls ; and few things, Arabella,
are more curious or striking than the
machines which convey the prisoners from
thence to the Court-House to take their trials.
The wheels of this machine are fourteen feet at
least high, and under the axletree is suspended
a wooden cage, sufficiently large to contain a
couple of culprits, perforated with air holes to
preserve them from suffocation ; and in this
miserable plight, guarded both before and behind by seapoys, they are exhibited to the
eyes of the populace—the whole of which
has to me a very distressing appearance.
There is but one court for civil and criminal
causes, though the judges are three in number ;
and an Armenian always attends as interpreter between the Court and the plaintiff, or
defendant, on all occasions. Moreover, the
Company have a linguist entertained in their
service, who is a Baronet, and receives a liberal gratuity for the exercise of his knowledge
of those languages, so essential to their

commercial interests. The Esplanade, like those several royal parks, St. James's, the Green, and Hyde Park, answers manifold purposes of convenience and pleasure to the Europeans.

For the Esplanade contains, besides the race ground, many shady and delightful spots ; the roads also to the Fort, to Watson's Works, etc., etc., lie through it ; and is often frequented by moonlight, by elegant walking parties, notwithstanding both the Company's and the Governor's gardens are always open for polite resort, and contain articles of vegetation of the first beauty and value, and every other mark of taste and happy cultivation.

You will naturally suppose, that statuary is a species of garden ornament the Governor and Company are not unmindful of ; but to give you a list of the characters introduced is a task I shall not undertake. I had, indeed, a scheme for immortalizing you and Doyly, could I have only brought you together on this spot ; for, superadded to a Milton, who

Into the heaven of heavens, &c., &c.

your figure should have represented the Allegro, his the Penseroso, of that sublime poet.

But I thank Mr. Emson's tyranny, and your want of affection for Sophia Goldsborne, that so happy a thought must remain unexecuted. I trifle, Arabella, with my pen, when my heart is dejected ; but I beg you will consider that dejection as one of those many follies human nature is surprised into, when pleasure, by too long enjoyment, has lost the power to please ; and that, like another Alexander, weeping for the discovery of unconquered worlds, we weep for want of some new amusements.

Landscapes, ruins, and every rural, every interesting *et cætera*, are much admired at Calcutta, as garden decorations ; and I visit a lady who is mistress of a spot, that is a close copy of Mrs. Southgate's beautiful lawns, parterres, and displays of agriculture, which meet the eye at her villa in the neighbourhood of Chertsey.

Did I ever yet tell you, that dreams and omens are much attended to by the natives of Calcutta—and that they have their lucky and unlucky days, which they observe with the same religious deference, as the most superstitious European of us all.

The well-bred and well-informed affect to ridicule these attentions ; but I can clearly perceive, that there are few minds uninfluenced by them—and, if you would do me strict justice, separate me not from the number—for when I dream of my father, or you in particular, I am either animated or depressed, according to the agreeable or terrific sensations with which I awake. Is this a proof of affection or weakness? I own to you, I wish to be flattered by you on the subject; and let me not be disappointed.

I have told you, the outside of the houses are white—but I find bricks are made at Calcutta; and therefore, unless washed by the composition called Chinam, I have been too hasty in my conclusions; for it was my idea, that the walls consisted merely of a clayey kind of substance, or of lath and plaster; so little defence is necessary against the climate.

When the hot winds are abroad, the angel of death, Arabella, is busy in all quarters; and, though numbers survive, the devastations are awful. Then is existence only supportable in the morning and evening; and the whole European people droop the head, and dissolution solely occupies their thoughts. I shall infect you, unless I hasten to tell you, I am,

Your's, etc.

S. G.

LETTER XXXI.

MOORSHEDABAD is the place at which the nabob of Bengal formerly kept his court, and which I, on that account, have a strange curiosity to visit. Our late Governor resided there, in the bosom of esteem and respect, even at the time when contests were deciding between the Company's servants and his *Mightiness* on the sword's point; and near this city is the Gentoo university I have already mentioned. I find myself very dull— but opiates are sometimes as salutary as cordials, and common life does not unremittingly supply us with great or astonishing incidents.

It is rather *mal-a-propos*—but no matter— I will, while it is fresh in my memory, tell you, that the natives wear arm-bracelets; and, as a proof of my remembrance of you, I have enabled myself, on my return, to present you with a pair of no contemptible value.

It is my intention (though perhaps it may surprise you) on my return to England, to visit all places of polite resort in such magnificent apparel, as may bespeak the splendour and the dignity of my Eastern connections and obtain me first-rate consequence in my native country. For, unless I bear the marks of travelled knowledge about me, who will be inclined to give me the superiority I am so justly entitled to, over those who have never travelled at all ?

———

THE Conscious Lovers is a piece I read with displeasure (at least some scenes of it) and behold represented with disgust : Sir Richard Steele is in general both a chaste and a moral writer ;—and how such a character could be capable of drawing a Cimberton, with all his *outré* licentiousness about him, is to me a problem beyond the power of the present age to resolve.

However, to spare the author, I will advert to the performers of this comedy. The Rosetta of Love in a Village with elegance and propriety sustained the part of Indiana ; and in Beville, a young gentleman recently arrived from China did himself great credit. Mrs. D——was so pleased with him, that she invited him to her house, as did also the Hartlys, and my father honoured him with so much notice, that I began to fear he would outstrip poor Doyly in his approbation ; but let him do his best, I will not be found an unfaithful friend to the absent. Should he chuse to admire me, he has my consent ; but for a serious attachment he must excuse me.

You complain, Arabella, that instead of enabling you, in fancy, to trace out my voyage to India step by step, and enter into my amusements and surprises—that the first of my letters is dated Bengal Bay, and all my succeeding ones are filled with anecdotes and descriptions of Calcutta. I assure you, it is not my fault that you are not better informed ; for I wrote you every particular I could suppose would amuse you, from Madras, and did believe it would be safely transmitted to you. However, since you so much desire it, I will endeavour to recollect the few observations I had an opportunity of making, and adventures I met with, before I reached this land of gallantry and politeness.

The first port we touched at on our passage was the Madeiras, which I need not tell you, is an African island, in the hands of the Portuguese. It consists, chiefly, of a wonderful rock, the surface of which is a continuation of vine-yards, fruitful beyond credibility ; and though our stay was short, we made a visit to the Governor, whose house is situated on such an eminence that we laboured hard to attain it : but, the eminence attained, our reception and entertainment well rewarded our trouble.

The principal town is Funchall : but so much has already been said of this place by other voyagers, and I will only mention a dexterous and critical manœuvre, performed by the Portuguese ; for, by means of the surf, on your quitting the island, boats are shot to a distance from the shore, that is like enchantment ; and though dangerous, is seldom known to be fatal, these people being so perfectly acquainted with the business. Here we took in some pipes of that wine which receives its name from the island ; and it is not improbable, on their return to England, (having twice doubled the Cape, and acquired the perfection believed derivable from that circumstance) but you may drink my health in some part of it, when circulated through your metropolis by the wine-merchant to whom it is consigned.

From the starting of some of our water casks, we brought to in the harbour of St. Johanne, a small island, inhabited by black people only, who, from a species of whimsical pride, are ambitious of being employed, though in the meanest offices, by the English. Amused

with the singularity of their humour, I suppose, some of the ship's crews, that have visited them, have made them understand the
dignity and consequence of Dukes and Mar-
quisses, etc., etc., in the British empire ; for,
ludicrous as you may conceive it, our water
casks were filled and rolled to and from the
shore by a Lord Duke, and three Earls, of the
first titles you are acquainted with ; together
with a whole illustrious progeny of sons and
daughters around, soliciting equal honours in
our service.

At St. Helena, I was much struck by the
transparency of the water at the mouth of the
harbour, to the depth of upwards of thirty
fathoms, which flows over black rocks, that
are as visible to the eye, as if barely beneath
the surface.

At Bombay, the Company have a dock, and
a most capacious harbour ; to which place of
safety the India ships make their periodical
return ; for, though the mountains Balagant
(which run the length of the peninsula, within
the Ganges) are so high as to check the western monsoons, yet is the Coromandel coast
in no degree fitted to be the station of ships,
beyond a certain time.

I was ashore at Madras—the Governor's boat being sent off for our conveyance which is well built and manned. But the boats are, all of them, merely boards lashed together by a kind of thongs, made of some vegetable substances; the thongs passing through holes bored for that purpose and stopped by chinam.

Their appearance is unwieldy; nor are they so well calculated to bear the sea, having flat bottoms, as those of a different construction; on which account, it is no unfrequent thing for them to be swamped, that is filled by water and sunk, with all on board, to the utmost depth of the harbour. They are manned by six Blacks, one of whom steers, and one watches the waves; for, to speak in the nautical language, what they have successively to encounter, are the surfs, and a lull; and, during the last calm moment, they pull with all their might, and then prepare themselves to combat the violence of the former. The passengers, however, when acquainted with the laws of the place, take a sousing with great composure; for, should one single European be lost by a swamp, all the poor Blacks belonging to the boat are put to death; they are, therefore, certain of being fished up with safety and dexterity, with no worse consequence than spoiling their clothes and, of course, preventing their figuring away on the island.

The Governor's house is a handsome building, and his entertainment of strangers liberal. The island consists of two towns, called, from the complexion of their inhabitants, the White and Black Towns. The name of Fort St. George is so seldom used, that it is almost forgot—it is under the civil, and every other regulation of Calcutta. Of the Cape I shall not speak —though I was regaled with some of the wine so called, whilst we lay off Table Bay—so much has been written by persons of taste and information, respecting the beauty of the country. We were treated with an illumination, very surprising in its appearance from fire insects, which overspread the surface of the water ; and, though prepared for it by report, I did not marvel the less on beholding it. The Line, I need not tell you, is twice crossed in an East India voyage, and many phœnomena are encountered ; such as its raining on each side of the ship, without one drop falling upon the deck ; of which I, your friend, was a spectator, with alternate squalls and calms, that startle a fresh-water

sailor ; and this is all I can remember, unin-
serted in a multitude of authors, who have
either been eye-witnesses of what they relate
or received their accounts from good authority.
The tempests of the Cape, are, in general,
frightful ; but so prosperous were our gales
that Neptune's domain has no terrors for my
recollection, experienced in my own person
—though I tremble at every breeze, on account
of those to which my perhaps less fortunate
friends may be exposed.

Mrs. Hartly has sent to inform me, by Miss
Rolle, that a resolution has just now been carried, *nem. con.*, by the company assembled
in the saloon, with my father's highest approbation, to deprive me of the use of pen, ink,
and paper, during my future residence at Bengal. Which will they punish most, Arabella,
you or me ? I leave you to decide, (as you
best know how far my literary labours are
pleasing, and imagine yourself competent to
declare the degree of pleasure I receive therefrom) whilst I attend this tribunal ; where I
am certain of creating more friends by a gra-
cious smile or two, than I shall find malecon-
tents from any article of conduct in your

S. G.

LETTER XXXII.

It is a common observation, Arabella, with moral writers, and the fact is literally true at Calcutta —that life is a chequered scene. The last ships that take their departure this season, are gone, and my levees are sensibly affected by the returns to Europe. But I am told the rule at Calcutta is to balance the regrets of absence by the pleasures of re-union.

"Do but conceive," says Mrs. Hartly, " what delight it will give you to renew these intermitted connections—to hear all the news from England—to receive fresh supplies of fashion—and, perhaps, " added she, with an agreeable look of meaning, " see Edmund Doyly again. "

I felt myself blush to a painful degree, as we were not alone ; for, if we had, I should not have attempted concealments, that would have been an insult on her penetration. She, however, kindly relieved me, by instantly changing the subject, and appearing unconscious of her triumph over my former reserves ; yet would it be much the wisest part in me to appoint a successor in my partiality—for my mind, Arabella, tells me, I shall see Doyly no more.

Young D——improves every hour, and
mixes in all our parties ; which is a proof of
one of Chesterfield's tenets, however apocry-
phal I hold them in general ; for, that we rise
or sink with our company, is undeniable. Example—precept—a sense of shame-—and a
desire to please, are great, I had almost said
infallible, polishers of the manners ; and we
become very decent copies of first rate originals,
unless incorrigible beings indeed, and incapable of feeling, and of distinguishing.

I am plunged into the utmost concern ; my
amiable Bramin, Arabella, died last night ;
and died, I am assured, blessing me. It seems
he took a fever, a few days ago, but my friends
were so kind, they kept it from my knowledge ;
and, on my father's Sekar presenting himself
this afternoon, with a woe-begone aspect, Mr.
Hartly drew him aside, as if on particular
business, and received from him the account
I have set before you. Gentle and benevolent spirit ! if it is permitted for mortal beings
to exercise thy care, and to be constituted
objects of thy kindness, deign to bestow a
thought on me !—O ! he was all that heaven
has ever condescended to make human nature
—and I will raise a pagoda to his memory in

my heart, that shall endure till that heart beats no more.

How will they dispose of his worthy remains? No funeral pile will, I hope, consume them to ashes—Yet wherefore that wish? for then will they be secure from every possibility of insult, or danger of mingling with dust less pure than their own.

I have, by my father, begged the Sekar to procure, if that indulgence is not incompatible with the Gentoo customs, a lock of his hair, for the purpose, my dear girl, of making it a mental talisman, like the poor monk's box and Yorick, against all the irregularities to which we Christians are subject. You want such a shield the least of any person I do or ever did know; yet, Arabella, you shall have a locket set with pearl, with some device suitable to the occasion, and wear it near your heart, for its virtues will be abundant.

My sensibility was, however, too much interested by this unexpected event for raillery to be reasonable, or good advice well timed; I therefore retired to my chamber, not, I fear, to sleep, but to reflect upon the transient gift of existence. Doyly will feel for me, if you mention this news to him, for much did he

honour and prize my Bramin and court his
favour. Doyly may nevertheless, even whilst
I am writing this name, have reached the
confines of eternity, and found the ocean as
merciless as the cruel disease to which our
favourite has fallen a victim. Peace, unending
peace, be with his shade! and, take notice,
that should time and chance restore me to
my country, I will erect a pagoda in Britain,
to perpetuate the remembrance to *my*, or,
what will be exactly the same thing, *your*
posterity, that so exemplary a character was on
the list of my Bengal acquaintance ; and that I
doubt not but I shall meet him, where parting
is an evil no longer to be apprehended ; and
sin and sorrow have no place. I would not,
Arabella, believe at this moment, that any
attachment he felt for me, was the cause of
the slightest pain to him, for the world—and
henceforth be all my vanity subdued. Tyrants
of every kind, are the terrors and disgrace
of their species, but the victories of vanity,
like those of the grand enemy of mankind,
are marked by devastation, and enjoyed without other delight than the delight of a malign
and baneful soul. I will, however, try to
be chearful.

Did I ever tell you, that the Calcutta ladies are passionately fond of jessamine and roses ? but such is the fact ; and moreover, if my recollection deceives me not, I called their bowers, *recesses*, for fear you should not understand so obsolete a term, at this refined period, in England. It was an absurdity of my own creation—for the celebrated bower of the celebrated Rosamond, at Woodstock, will give you some proper idea of the Eastern taste, in this respect ; some of them being wholly impervious to the sun-beam, and a most relieving situation, you may suppose, in such a climate as Bengal—at the same time that they are diffusing the most grateful odours around, and feasting the eye with an intermixture of the loveliest productions of nature ; and these bowers also, it is a settled point in my breast, will be introduced by me at my British villa ; not as an improvement, but a revolution in the ornamentals of gardens— and a proof, that when good sense bade adieu to my fair countrywomen, she fled on the wings of the winds to the Eastern shore ; and, should you, or your friends, be inclined to engage in her pursuit, you will find her, much at her ease, at Hartly Bungilo.

These are flights of fancy, I grant you—
mere creatures of the air I breathe ; but let
me once find myself set down safely on the
banks of the Thames, and I will endeavour
to convert them into realities ; of which you
would, I trust, become a glad spectator.

We are all of us oddly situated. Mrs. D——
is tired of India—but Mrs. D——cannot declare as much, without implying that she is
desirous of being a bride, the determined
consequence of her arrival here.—I sigh for
my Arabella's company, and would advance
the secret of Mrs. D——'s heart ; but that it
is very probable poor Doyly and I should then
meet on the high seas, and have the power
only of exchanging a passing look. My Father
has affairs to settle, he cannot so suddenly
bring to bear as he imagined—and is so fettered and so entangled by his own sublime ideas,
and the sublimity of his bride elect's sentiments, that he knows not which way to turn
himself. Moreover, should fate and fortune
send Doyly back—have not I a vow, like a
wall of brass, thrown up between us ? I will
only say thus much on the occasion—that
sentiment leads us frail and narrow-sighted
beings into more follies and perplexities than

any other rule of conduct whatever. We must
not, for example, make ourselves happy, if
not altogether consistent with sentiment;
we must not be sincere to those we love, unless
that sincerity can be reconciled to sentiment;
nor, on detecting ourselves guilty of an
egregious absurdity, dare to renounce it, unless
duly authorised by sentiment : so that sentiment, which is a thing amiable in itself, is
rendered the most pernicious of all things in
its effects ; and we live and die in the act of
sacrificing all that is truly valuable or amiable
in life to a chimera of our own brain ; which
we, like lunatics, dress up in the likeness of
sentiment. We laugh at the Gentoos, and
their plurality of gods—but truly ridiculous
our wisdom must appear, which, instead
of being exerted in the cause of happiness,
its whole end and aim is to teach us to be
miserable with a good grace, and undo the
benevolent work of Providence with our own
prophane hands : for, to be happy, not miserable, were we, most undoubtedly, created.

I will change my subject a second time—
for I can make nothing to my satisfaction,
or my reputation, of the one I am now
engaged in.

I am called by the natives, Belate Be Bee
—the English lady; for, however, low rated
in England, I am a sovereign princess here;
and, was I so inclined, could wring the hearts
of my dependents. But, in like manner with
yourself, Arabella, I love to see the human
countenance dressed in smiles of content, of
gratitude, of innocent pleasure. It is a
reproach of the severest kind, to a feeling of
temper, to have interrupted the felicity
of others.

Belate Sab is an Englishman; Chookalo
Calalo is a lighted candle: but I am forming
a vocabulary, with which I mean to present
you, that I may at least find one in England
able to understand the words I have taken
so much pains to acquire.

Beville, (for so he is universally called, in
honour of his excellent performance of that
character) visits much at Hartly House; and
those who profess the art of analysing, place
those visits to my account. If my conversation was half as agreeable to him as his is to
me, there might be danger at Calcutta; but
he has many connections that can supply my
place to him, though his well-stored mind
has no counter-part under this meridian. I

therefore measure time by the long minutes till his return.

My father observes me more than usual, as if he would read my most secret thoughts— I shrink not from his penetrating eye ; I know he is too generous to constrain me, and too well read in his daughter's thoughts, to mistake her wishes in any instance beyond the present moment.

I am courting Beville for *you ;* and he has already taught himself to dwell upon your praises. Is the picture you draw of your friend, Madam, a real or a flattered likeness ? Why do oceans roll between us ? Your letters of recommendation, what a high point of favour would they not procure for me ! I would make an immediate voyage to England, if I was possessed of such credentials, and to such a lady. Where it will end, I do not take upon me to say ; but the marks are at present strong about him, that whenever within the reach of you, he will make you a visit. Young D——, I perceive it, likes him not. I honour him for it, because it is not natural for us to love those who eclipse us ; and at dissembling, in this respect, he is a novice. When my Bramin was alive, I had a strange wild desire to out-

shine all my female acquaintance ; the desire
was unworthy of me, and as such has been
reprobated by me. I set my understanding
no longer out to shew—I spend no idle hours
at my toilet ; and am an interested participater
of all the gay scenes which I behold others
enjoy with rapture. You will be, perhaps,
for placing this change in my taste, temper,
and conduct, to a wrong cause ; but I **protest**
to you, Doyly's absence or presence is no part
of the question, at this precise period, in the
deranged breast of,

Your
S. G.

LETTER XXXIII.

THE Sekars, or Brokers, to whom the sale
of all kinds of merchandize is intrusted, have
an Ana, I understand, in every Rupee ; keep
three writers each ; and are, many of them,
masters of much wealth : but there is no doing
without them, and they generally preserve a
fair reputation. My father is, however, so
well satisfied with his Sekar, that he intends

making him a handsome present on his leaving India.

I was last night at the tragedy of *Zara*, and shed abundance of tears. The poet has indeed created a distressing conflict for a youthful heart, that has a powerful effect on the feelings ; and I think, Arabella, the constitution of my mind is such, that I should have fell a victim to the parental injunction. What abundant reason have I not, therefore, to be thankful for my happy condition ! for I am not more anxious for my freedom of choice in the article that must determine the colour of my future life (I mean the choice either of a single or a married situation) than my father is anxious in all things for my felicity ; and I am as little desirous of bestowing myself contrary to my father's approbation, as I should be reluctant to do violence to my own inclination ; which I indeed consider as the natural rights of existence.—I have sat for my picture, to oblige Mrs. Hartly, but have enjoined her to let it remain in Calcutta, and not suffer her friendship to lead her into the error of believing, because I may hold a tolerable first-rate place in her heart, that she is entitled to introduce my resemblance into her closet

at Hartly Bungilo, where I should disgrace
her collection.

It requires no small talents, Arabella, to
prevent our heads being the dupe of our hearts.
We esteem an object, and we will, for argu-
ment's sake, allow the object to be estimable ;
but the character is a private one, and its
beauties and its virtues have neither influence
or operation beyond the small circle of friendship; and consequently, though to us very
striking and great, would become ridiculous
by being brought forward to universal admiration, like a taper in the sun-beam. And, I
pray you, who am I, Sophia Goldsborne, that
I should be found amongst the most accomplished of my sex—who want not the aid of a
foil to palliate the folly of my obtaining a
niche ?—I should die with confusion at such
a violation of common sense and common
decorum.

I have made an acquaintance with a Mrs.
Savage, the gentlewoman who keeps a boarding-school at Calcutta, and find her very well
qualified for so arduous an undertaking; for
her morals are good, and her understanding
cultivated. She sighs, however, she confesses,
like myself, for her native country ; and will,

I doubt not, as soon as she is able, return to
England. The loss Calcutta must sustain
on such an event taking place, has made me
cast about for a successor : and I hoped Mrs.
Rider might have been prevailed upon ; but
she modestly declines, saying, there is a great
difference between the education of children
under the parental roof, and in a situation
that renders you answerable at all points for
their safety and welfare ; an undertaking no
abilities are equal to ; for, in such a situation,
you must depend upon others, who may
either abuse or betray their trust, and defeat
the   best-formed,   and   the   honest-executed
plan, as far as respects the superior on earth.

There are, however, in England, my good
girl, many accomplished and slenderly provided for women, with more courage than Mrs.
Rider possesses, that might be induced, by
the knowledge of the great advantages derivable from the exercise of their talents at
Calcutta, to make the voyage. Will you put
the knowledge, therefore, into circulation ?
for no one article of female provision or accommodation can be of half the importance
as the happy direction of the mind and
manners, at the period when impressions are

most lively and indelible. For I would chal-
lenge my whole sex, by an appeal to their
own experience, to disprove this assertion, so
well understood by Pope, and so worn in the
public eye by quotation—

For as the twig is bent, the tree's inclined.

And so much has the worthy and amiable
Mrs. D——her good wishes in this cause, that
she has offered to be a subscriber to any
established fund for making it an object
with an accomplished Englishwoman to spend
one seven years of her life at Calcutta, and
to ensure a valuable candidate for the vacan-
cies as they may occur.

My father has purchased a spot for a Bungilo. I was low spirited at the information,
it seemed so strongly to imply our prolonged
residence in India. Mrs. D——has had the
goodness, however, to let me into a secret;
for my father intends it as a compliment to
Miss Hartly on her becoming Mrs. D——,
with the permission, nevertheless, of him and
his friends to visit, whilst he is within reach
of such visitation.

How variable is human opinion !—this intelligence constituted that very act a pleasure,

which, while its motives were unascertained, excited much pain—and here am I, entering, with my whole powers, into its decoration and embellishment.—Adieu, my Arabella! I do not at this moment despair of our re-union.

S. G.

LETTER XXXIV. *

I HAVE exposed myself, Arabella, and every tongue in Calcutta is now employed in telling it. My father presented himself somewhat hastily, I thought, because unexpectedly, just as we were this day seated at dinner; and standing behind my chair, without the least preparation, said, "Poor Doyly is "—— and on some account, I did not observe what, stopped.

"Is what ? " cried I, with an emotion that surprised all the company. "O what, Sir, is poor Mr. Doyly ? " "Only, " replied my dear father, pressing my hand, " only arrived, within this ten minutes, safe at Calcutta. "

----

* The date of which is six months after the preceding one.

What a mortifying discovery has the interest I took in his safety occasioned !—Mrs. Hartly endeavours to sooth me into self-reconcilement, but, I think, it can never more take place. Infatuated girl !—but first impulses, I find, are not to be guarded against ; and the secret of my heart, which I have so long treasured up, has escaped me, irrecoverably escaped me ! "Where is the good gentleman, " said Mrs. Hartly, with a provoking turn of countenance, " shall we not be favoured with his company ? " "He is following me," replied my father, " with dispatches for Sophia, from her old friend and school-fellow ; the honour of presenting which he refused making a transfer of, or I should have had the delivering of them."

Doyly now entered, and with his usual grace bowed to the company ; who with one voice congratulated him on his return, except the foolish weak creature I need not name. His dress improved his appearance—I never saw anybody—abstracted from all superabundant partiality—look so well in deep mourning. An uncle, who stood between him and the possession of a fine estate, and who, with an unkindness that forbids all regret for his

decease, had compelled him to quit his native
country a mere adventurer, did not live to
reproach him, on his return to England, with
the madness (as he called it) of his East India
voyage, though solely resulting from the narrowness of his finances, and the consequential
unfavourableness of his prospects in life.
And (could you have supposed such a thing,
Arabella?) the young man's head, on this
change of fortune, became instantly giddy,
insomuch that, having got rid of his commission the first possible moment, he forgot every
earthly creature, and every earthly spot, except Calcutta, and some few friends there that
shall be nameless, and accordingly embarked,
with a heart I had marked down for some other
female's prize, in the first packet, in order
to lay that no less faithful than affectionate
heart at my feet ; and, delivering me back
my own packet, made every imaginable
apology for his sin of omission, etc., etc., on
the occasion.

And this wild act my father considers as a
token of violent regard, forbidding me, by
his looks and example, to shew any displeasure.
An exclamation, however, escaped me, that
sufficiently spoke my feelings :—" Not seen

my Arabella !—not giving her the satisfaction
of knowing I am alive ! or enabled yourself
to tell me a thousand pleasing particulars
where her welfare is concerned ! O Mr.
Doyly, is it possible ?'' '' Yes,'' replied my
father, in an accent that mortified me not a
little, '' it is, my dear Sophia, possible, that
poor Mr. Doyly is safe arrived at Calcutta.''

Wonderful all this !—nor do I foresee when
my wonder will cease. Now am I convinced
of the power of my charms, and shall want
no farther support in my own good opinion
for ever.

Mrs. D——'s reception of Doyly was, like
herself, engaging beyond what I can describe.
'' Our parties,'' said she, '' have been incom-
plete without you, and my *petits soupers*
devoid of animation. Remember, we never lose
you again at Calcutta ; nor will I open my doors,
unless you are to be one of the company.''

Young D——stared, and I enjoyed the
alarms this address visibly gave rise to in his
breast ; for at Calcutta, as I have repeatedly
told you, the idea of matrimony is insepar-
able from the knowledge of an acquaintance
between the sexes—and he seemed to anticipate
his downfall, should his mother-in-law take

a husband to herself, not much more than
his own age.

Mrs. D——saw the effect her good-humour
and friendship for Doyly had produced in the
selfish mind of her son ; and, to the entertainment of all present (for all present were soon
aware of her motive) coqueted with the young
man, until the hour for retirement arrived ;
but then thought proper to undeceive him, lest
any mischief between them should ensue ;—
for Mr. D——wears a sword—and who will
not grant, that a rival in interest, is as severe
a provocation, with some tempers, as a rival
in love ?—A pretty winding up, indeed, it
would have proved of Mr. Doyly's romantic
voyage, to have had his throat cut, from an
innocent frolic, in the hour of self-congratula-
tion and imagined security ! But that,
Arabella, is frequently found the hour of our
worst danger—and, of course, it is our duty
to be evermore on our guard.

But let me do Doyly justice, before I go
to sleep. He did, I find, enquire for you, agreeably to the superscription of my letters, but you
was gone into the country. He waited your
return, while patience, in his situation, was a
virtue—and did *intend*, but forgot to fulfil his

intention, to leave them in the care of your
servant, with a note of lamentation for the
disappointment he met with, in not meeting
with your fair self ;—and so the whole matter
is rather more decently accounted for than in
the first instant ; —for, let me bear witness,
when the heart is occupied by such fluctuating
subjects as the winds and waves, it is not
extraordinary the memory should be absorbed,
and the conduct vague and inconsistent. His
return would have given me tenfold pleasure,
if he had brought me news of my Arabella :—
but, from this state of the case, I think
he must be forgiven—What say you ?—
Aye or No !

Adieu.

O talk not to me of the wealth she possesses———

it seems, was the language of Doyly, on my
father's attempting to make a long speech
relative to what he intended to give me :—and
thus you find me on the edge of the matrimonial precipice ;—for, though tender distress,
and delicate embarrassment, are very pretty
decorations for *painted* scenes—the realities
of life need receive no such colourings from

the pencil—for the sensible head, and the sympathising heart, feels them all ;—I shall, therefore, say not one word how I looked, or how I replied, when solicited by the man of my choice, on the one hand, to accept him, and commanded by my father, on the other hand, to follow my own inclinations. Generous, indulgent command !—for well was he acquainted with the bent of my inclinations, before such command was issued—the Padra, therefore, stands a good chance of obtaining some twenty gold mohrs, at least, on my account—but I will have the whole affair as private as possible, let my friends remonstrate as they may.

Lord Cornwallis is on his way to Calcutta, to assume the reins of government. That he is a man of fashion, we hear without emotion ; —but that we hear he is a man of abilities and honour, we rejoice. He will be received with every mark of distinction, in honour of his and our Sovereign ; but his hour of departure alone will evince the advance he has made in our approbation and attachment. I stand impartial, and will give his claims due weight ; —but, if it should be required of me to forget the Governor I have known, and sink his fame

in the celebrity of any new comer, I shall beg
to be excused. Hereditary advantages, however, brilliant their effects, are but secondary
recommendations ;—the self-ennobled individual, and him who disgraces not the memory
of his illustrious forefathers, being the only
highly revered characters in this land of commerce and plain understanding.

I am, etc., etc.,
Your's,
S. G.

LETTER XXXV.

AMAZEMENT !—so this same little winning
Mr. Doyly, is the godson of my beloved mother,
and your near relation. A pretty plot this !
—and may I lose my pretensions to the privileges of a Christian female, if I pardon your
share in it —or, what is tantamount, be compelled to embrace the narrow and illiberal
faith of the sons of Omar ; which by the way,
I have now some thoughts of doing—for I
shall, at least, be of consequence whilst living,
if annihilation (in the opinion of my adorers)

must be my portion when dead ;—and that
is more than my professed friends, though of
the race of believers, have chose to give me,
in this instance. The following is the confession the offending parties in the East have been
brought to make ; nor shall I fail to add your's
thereto, the first opportunity by which it can
be obtained.

My father, perceiving me inclined to marry
in the East, for wealth, etc., with men old
enough to make me guilty, in so doing, of
a breach of the canonical articles, which
positively forbid your marrying your grandfather ;—and anxious to unbend *tête-a-tête*
with a son-in-law likely to make his daughter
happy—writes off to England for Doyly, telling him, if his prospects were not improved,
he believed he could promise to be serviceable
to him in India. Doyly embarks, and, being
arrived, receives the offer, point blank, of his
friend's daughter, with all her emoluments
and endowments, provided her consent could
be obtained ; in which attempt he was to have
all lawful aid and assistance.

Doyly (as who would not) snaps at the offer
A young damsel of my claims and appearance
might, Arabella, have been carried with

success, to a much higher market ;—but every man in his humour, say I—and, being my father's property, he had a right to indulge his fancy, as far as it was reconcileable to my wishes.

Doyly began his manœuvrings, I suppose nothing doubting ; for where is there a young man in this age to be found, that thinks humbly of himself—person or mind ?— when lo ! what should come to pass, but his imbibing so exalted an idea of the height and depth of my deservings, that he falls into the state of boobyism, which caused all my suspense, folly, etc., etc.,—for, though his respect for my mental merits was abundant, from repeated conversations with you, our common friend, thereon—yet, not having seen me, within my remembrance, my personal graces (which were to be superadded to the account) were so dazzling and so dismaying, that he very childishly gives away his heart, without seeking a return in kind ;—and no less childishly resolves never to disclose his tender absurdity, until some change, or chance, had lifted him a few degrees nearer an equality with me in pecuniary matters ;—a resolution that locked up his lips, not only in all the

intercourse he enjoyed with me (and encouragement to speak out, I fear, was legible
in my countenance, had translating looks
been his talent) but, in the moment also of
bidding adieu, when presumption is so ex-
cusable, because so natural in a lover—who
knows not what he does or says, until his
offended Dulcinea recalls him, by her anger, to
a sense of his crime, and he begs pardon, and
offends—and offends, and begs pardon, to the
last point of the last interview between them.

But, to shew you the metamorphosis riches
can produce—this timid, humble Doyly, is
become the most ardent and precipitate of
lovers—and would have seized my hand,
nolens volens, the first evening of his arrival
at Calcutta ; in consequence, however, I should
add, of the universal opinion (with my father
at the head of that opinion) that I entertained
a secret *tendre* for him.—Secret, do I call it ?
—that ever falsehood and deceit should look
so well upon paper !—but, bound by the laws
of decorum to preserve such secrets inviolate,
that should, Arabella, by the courtesy of our
friends, be deemed a secret, which has not
been confessedly revealed, whatever presump-
tive evidence is producible of the contrary.

And yet, there is something premature in
the business ;—for who knows what friends
Lord Cornwallis may bring over with him to
make one repent one's yieldingness of temper ?—I have, however, placed the emblems
of tranquil feelings before me (the devices I
mentioned to you, wrought with the hair of
my departed Bramin) in order to extinguish
the embers of vanity, now re-kindling in my
heart :—yet what have I to ask of quiet-mind-
edness, more than I possess ?—for, Arabella,
I am content to leave Calcutta, without
occasioning one scene of blood and slaughter
in. my name, under the spreading branches
of the trees of destruction (which might have
been so reasonably expected from my charms)
in contest for the honour of my hand ; and am
preparing myself (with my own consent) to
domesticate in Britain, to the very confines
of oblivion—which is carrying the virtue of
humility to a most unprecedented height,
in a damsel of my complexion and turn
of sentiment.

The same round of amusements is about
to take place, as at this time last year. The
Gentoo holidays begin first—the races succeed
—and the theatre will open some weeks sooner

than at that period ;—all things being thus
early in a proper train, out of compliment,
I suppose, to the expected Governor—so that
we shall not want amusement ;—and I have
it in contemplation to point out a few dramatic characters to Doyly, which, I persuade
myself, he would fill in a manner far from
disgraceful to either me or himself. Calcutta
once more looks like itself ;—men, Arabella,
in other words, abound ; —and I am beheld by
all my old acquaintance, as if I had horns on
my head, because I have not renounced my
maiden state ;—but the mystery will soon be
unravelled, and they will find, that though
wealth could not tempt me, modest merit,
noble mindedness, and a long list of matrimonial requisites, could prevail, even over a
vow—a vow you can produce against me,
to the impeachment of my morals, and the
discolouring of my lily-white fame ;—for,
amongst my other articles of celebrity, my
sincerity of heart, and the sincerity of my lips
(or, as you would call it, veracity) have a distinguished place. I thank you for your kind
remembrance of me, and shall conceive every
cause lost, in which you may choose to accept
a brief—so prevailing are the reasons you have

set before me, in excuse for Doyly's conduct
—not to mention a word of the force of
example—for you, Arabella, forgive him
neglects, I could not hope you to pardon.

I am your's, etc.,
S. G.

LETTER XXXVI.

LORD CORNWALLIS is hourly expected, and
bugeros are in readiness to fall down the
Hughley, on its being announced he has made
the mouth of the Ganges.

Mrs. D——, with an ardour I did not think
her capable of, has fitted herself and friends
out at all points, to do this great man honour
—at least, by adding one more bugero to his
train ; and my father says, our company cannot be dispensed with.

What can I say ?—my spirits are in unison
with the occasion ;

My shepherd is kind and my heart is at ease

But I shall not be without my apprehensions ;
—for, did I not see the time, when Doyly's

life was in imminent danger, though on a
party of pleasure :—but Doyly promises to
be discreet, and Mr. Emson has taken himself to England ;—I will, therefore, speak
peace to my fears, and gratify Mrs. D——'s
desire of exhibiting me. But of Mrs. D——I
have somewhat to mention, not quite so much
in the style of friendship as I had expected ;
she can have her concealments, as well as a
certain young Lady, when she pleases—for
(could you have thought it) my father's will,
which he put into her hands to peruse, when
she was about to make her own, contained
his approbation of Doyly for a son-in-law—
his act of sending for him from England, for
the purpose of gaining my favour—and a
solemn request, that she would finish what he
had begun, provided it was discovered to be
my inclination. A pretty business, truly !—
and thus, it is probable, she will be often employed by him, in secret services respecting
his child, that will be preconcerted between
them. I would be angry, if I could resist
being pleased—but, next to yourself, Arabella,
she is the wisest and the best creature on earth.
—Mrs. Hartly is not forgot by me—nor her
sweet disposition unremembered. She has,

however, a family to share her attentions and
kindnesses ; whereas Mrs. D—— is ours entirely, and without alloy.

One of our visiting friends has taken a
French leave of us. I believe I have told you,
that one side of the river Hughley is priviledged
ground, the opposite shore to Calcutta, to which
place this young spark is fled. He spent his
evening, I find, in the tavern, at the gaming-
table, where, having lost considerable sums,
he was pushed on from one act of desperation
to another, until, not being worth a shilling,
he was compelled to become a fugitive among
fugitives (for no one of good prospects or good
connections resides there) the fatal and frequent consequence of this dreadful infatua-
tion. Card-playing was designed for amuse
ment only, to unbend the mind from too
intense reflection. It has, however, been
perverted into an engine of destruction—a
calamity without a mitigation—for what re-
sources has a wretch in his hour of self-created
affliction, when the whole world, and his own
heart, are united in his condemnation ? The
gamester, moreover, seldom falls alone ; an
amiable wife; a lovely offspring, are too often
involved in the crushing misfortune ; and such

is the nature of his profession, that even success ought to wound his feelings, for he must, Arabella, undo, if he is not undone.

I am, nevertheless, so much interested in the fate of this young sinner, that I have besought Doyly to serve him if he can—for he is the victim of premature, of unbounded prosperity;—had he been less, he would have been much more fortunate. We shall therefore make a point of procuring him some moderate re-establishment, which, we trust, he will be smarted into a knowledge of the value of, and game no more.

Lord C—— is arrived, and professed himself much pleased with his reception.

Every creature is flying to his house to pay their *baise-mains ;* and it is said, that as soon as the bustle is over, the Nabob will make him a public visit. There will be a sight, Arabella, for an European gentlewoman ! How lucky it is, my hour for embarking did not arrive previous to this grand raree-show !

Our voyage was a pleasant and delightful one—for when the surface is smooth, I am fond of water excursions—and, by what you London people experience in your parties to and from Vauxhall, etc., etc., you may judge

how musical accompaniments must increase
the pleasure of the Eastern voyaging.

Young D—— has a good voice, and, what
I should never have suspected him of, sings
with much taste. We had an awning of
kittesaws, and did our best to be noticed when
the Bugero of bugeros passed us ; but, mortifying so ever as the confession may be, it shall
be confessed that I verily believe we were
confounded with the multitude.

My father has furnished himself with large
assortments of Eastern manufactures, by much
the largest part of which is intended for a
present to my friend, so that you stand a
chance of eclipsing all the Misses of your acquaintance—a most sentimental gratification :
but as for my part, *simplex munditiis* shall be
my motto, which requires as much skill to hit
off, without being under or over dressed in
a single article, as any female etiquette I know.
Moreover, so altered am I in my views and
wishes, that I have settled with myself to
affect the Gentoo air, which is an assemblage
of all the soft winning graces priests or poets
have yet devised a name for, and Doyly shall
figure away as my Bramin ; and so well have
I instructed him in every humane tenet of

that humane religion, that he will not hurt a
butterfly, nor can he dispatch even a troublesome musketto without a correspondent pang
—and habit, you know, is said to give us a
kind of second nature ;—but it is to do Mr.
Doyly barely justice to say, that no savage
climate, not even the climate of his, mine, or
your ancestors, has power to render him aught
but the friend of all created nature, and the
universal admirer of all Nature's productions ;
—but, as Sterne says, I am not celebrating the
man, but the sentiment.

We are to have a fishing party next week
for the participation of which amusement
nature has disqualified me by a painful degree
of sensibility ; for I cannot call by the name of
pleasure what must be purchased at the high
price of the suffering or death of any thing that
exists. This was the first attaching feature
my still-lamented Bramin discovered in my
mental character. You are, said he, "Madam,
a Christian by profession, but a Gentoo by
nature ; you would have done honour to the
religion of Brumma.'' They refused me not,
as I apprehended, a lock of this saint's
hair, and I have had it elegantly set for his
sake. He merited no less a compliment,

in return for his unfeigned approbation
of me.

It is got abroad, that we mean soon to leave
Bengal ; and here I have it, under the hand
and seal of one of my adorers, that broken
constitutions, and broken hearts, will be the
consequence of my departure ; for that those
who do not die of grief, will send themselves
speedily to their graves by libations to Neptune
for my safety. This, in your sober judgment,
may be deemed carrying gallantry to excess ;
but there have been instances of facts to the
full as extravagant, some years ago ;—the
Eastern world is, however, much improved,
and their errors corrected.

A generation of European children (if you
will give such an Irishism your passport, when
you observe that I mean children born in the
Eastern world) grow up daily, whose natural
endowments are excellent, and their education wonderful for this distant land ; so that,
instead of languishing, as formerly, the European ladies, and receiving with rapture the
hands of such as have the courage to brave
all the perils of the ocean to obtain them a
husband, and arrive with their credentials from
the Company in their hands ;—wives are now

chosen, by men of nice feeling, from among
these India-born ladies, (through natural in-
timacies, and a knowledge of their tempers,
manners, and conduct) in preference to these
adventurers. Yet is there no rule without an
exception—so that if you will be prevailed
upon, Arabella, to make an East India voyage,
I will engage a genius of my acquaintance,
who has repeatedly celebrated my small merits,
both in prose and verse, to present you
a congratulatory address upon your arrival,
and will ensure you a host of admirers.

You will, I fancy, be convinced by my trifling, I am no love-sick nymph—no, Arabella !
so far from it, that though it is not unlikely I
may marry Doyly, in obedience to my father's
commands, you must do me the justice to
acknowledge I bore his absence like a heroine
and seldom or ever made him the subject-
matter of my letters to England. I have
managed, however, to my father's satisfaction,
and have taught myself to despise your mali-
cious smiles ;—yet, on recollection, before 'it
is given me to embrace my Arabella, by being
made the young man's lawful wife, it may be
more for my credit to confess, than deny the
tender sentiments with which he inspired me.

In Calcutta, I believe, Hymen is seldom known to be attended at the nuptial ceremony by Cupid (for it is who bids most that wins the prize) ; and whilst the fair lady's person appertains to one happy man alone, her conversation is at the service of all those who have sufficient interest to get themselves introduced to her ; and the husband is so complaisant as to ask no questions.

Your's, etc.,
S. G.

LETTER XXXVII.

ALAS, Arabella, I am undone ! I have beheld so brilliant, so divine a spectacle—am so dazzled, and so captivated, and, like Gulliver in the land of Lilliput, find all the objects around me so diminutive and so mean, that I overlook and disregard them at every point. You will perceive, by this exordium, the Nabob has made his intended visit to the new Governor, and has carried off the heart of your unfortunate friend ;—but I will endeavour to conquer and regulate my feelings.

From Chitpore, the Nabob's palace, to
Calcutta, I have already told you is four miles ;
from whence such a procession as I must
never hope to behold again, proceeded to the
Esplanade, and that at a very early hour
in the morning.

His guards, on the occasion, were no less in
number than his whole battalion of black
troops, fine-looking fellows—and their complexions gave a grandeur to the scene. Their
uniform and their turbans were new, and
their fire-arms glittering bright ; and I would
have given the world on the instant to have
been a Nabobess, and entitled to so magnificent a train.

I whispered Doyly, and asked him what
he thought of the London sights in such a
moment ? He shook his head with due contempt, but made no reply, as we were surrounded by those who would have taken umbrage
at the most distant reflection (though in the
voice of truth) on England.

Seven elephants of the first magnitude were
led by their keepers, in like manner as our
sumpter-horses ; seated on the back of one
of which, on a throne of indescribable splendour, was his Nabobship, with a man behind

him, holding a superb fan, in the very act of
collecting the breezes in his service.

The throne was composed of gold, pearls,
and brilliants, and the Nabob's dress worth
a sovereignty ; nor was ever animal more
grandly caparisoned than the no less honoured
than exalted elephant on which he rode.

His state-palanquin followed, and was by
much the most desirable object my eyes ever
encountered, and differently built to those
used by the Europeans. Four pillars of massy
silver supporting the top, which was actually encrusted by pearls and diamonds ; and,
instead of verandas, fine glass plate on every
side, as well as the back and front, to shew his
Mightiness's person, I suppose, to the greatest advantage.

I was stationed nearly on a level with the
throne as it passed along ;—and judge, Arabella, if you can, of the ambitious throbs my
heart experienced, when I saw the Nabob's
eyes, sparkling with admiration, fixed on my
face ! Doyly turned pale, and the procession
advanced—yet were my charms unforgotten by
him ; for he twice or thrice looked back, and
constituted me the envy of the women, and
the torture of the men ; in a word, my

conquest was as evidence as the noon-day sun :
and who could dream of a mortal female's
refusing an enthroned adorer, with the wealth
of the Indies at his feet ?

Down knelt the half-reasoning animal, at
the entrance of the Governor's house, for his
illustrious master to alight ;—so powerful, yet
so docile !—so gentle, yet so terrific in appearance ! I am dying, Arabella, to have
one of these very Elephants at my command.

Breakfast was prepared for this princely
guest, at the Governor's ;—from whence he
was conducted across the Esplanade, to the
New Fort, where the troops were drawn out,
to compliment him with an exhibition of
their martial manœuvrings ; and he was shewn,
with apparent astonishment, to how great a
distance bomb-shells can be thrown.   He was
accompanied by the Governor's *Aid-de-camp*,
the whole day—expressed much delight on
viewing the camp at Bugee Bugee—but returned to Chitpore to dinner, the peculiar
customs of his religion not admitting of his
mixing with the Europeans, on that occasion.   Many of the officers were invited to his
palace, and sumptuously entertained, in an
adjoining apartment ; and in the evening,

some beautiful fire-works were played off in the garden of Chitpore—and the company returned much satisfied with his liberal and courteous demeanour.

I thought of Lady Wortley Montague's account of her being noticed by the Grand Seignor, when spectator of a Turkish procession, on the Nabob's observation of me ;—but there was this difference between the circumstances—namely, that the attention the Sultan paid that Lady was merely *en passant ;* whereas this Nabob of Nabobs proved, in the face of all the people, how long he bore me in mind—that is, how deeply he was wounded— and I hold myself in expectance of hearing more of him.

The return of the procession was with the same ceremonies—and I have dreamed alone of state palanquins, thrones, elephants, and seapoys ever since.

My friends, who visited the Fort, and traced the Nabob's steps wherever he went, tell me, a ship now on the stocks, at Watson's Works, of three decks (the first ever built at Calcutta) will be launched in a few days, and receive the name of the Earl Cornwallis, in honour of our Governor.—It will, no doubt, be a brilliant day ;—but whether it will be thought safe to trust me to be a spectator, or not, lest the Nabob should form plans for carrying me off, is uncertain, until I have heard the opinion of my male friends. That Doyly was frightened, is most certain ;—but an English-woman was not born to fear giant knights, or enchanted castles ; and the more especially, where an army would stand forth in her protection and defence. It would flatter my vanity to find them alarmed.—Ha ! ha ! ha ! Arabella—did you ever imagine your friend would make so magnificent a conquest ?— Poor Doyly, how small he has felt himself ever since !—Forgive my folly—I recollect my Bramin, and am myself again.

I am affectionately, your's
S. G.

LETTER XXXVIII.

Bless me, Arabella, how different objects can appear to different optics —My father talks of nothing but going to England, or

Doyly but of becoming a bridegroom.—"Softly, my dear Sir," said I to him, "for there are a few preliminary articles to be adjusted before that great event can take place.—If my father marries not in India, I will follow his example; and so, if you chuse to make it a concern of yours, get him to appoint his day, and that, I promise you, shall be mine."

We shall be a fine party of us, in crossing the ocean —for, Mr. and Mrs. Hartly, and the children, Mrs. Rider, and young Mr. and Mrs. D——, will accompany us;—letters having arrived, that require Mr. Hartly's personal attendance in England, and he will not leave his family behind.

Mrs. D——has been reproaching me, in the severest terms, for my treatment of Doyly. —Unkind ·Mrs. D——! I never thought it possible for you to chide in so serious a manner. —She says I shall distress my father beyond measure, by requiring what cannot be complied with.

"And why not, Mrs. D——," said I, interrupting her, "why not, I beseech you?— If a union *is* to take place between my father and you, wherefore should you embark for England previous thereto?—or, if it can be

necessary to observe such delay, why should
you set yourself in array against a compliment
I propose making you, of delaying my nuptials
also, until the air of my native country gives
me sufficient resolution to constitute Mr. Doyly
my sovereign lord ?—Methinks he shews great
impatience to assume the husband. ''

Mrs. D——walked off in a great state—the
first fit of the pouts I have ever seen her fall
into ; and who will give the second lecture
on the subject, I am at a loss to conjecture.—
Perhaps your eloquent little friend, my intended—you understand me, Arabella— but I
shall not allow it lawful for him to plead in his
own cause.—His reports will be so partial
his representations so—Ah, Arabella, I hear
my father ask for me !—what will become
of me ?

I have great powers, my good girl— and I
stood in need of their utmost exertion, when
opposed, as they have been, to Mrs. D——'s
best performance. I acknowledge her to be
a great actress, and only inferior to your friend,
who has carried her point, to all intents and
purposes ; and not a word more is to be mentioned—until the Padra receives his instructions to fill his purse in our service.—I do not

suppose, Arabella, that the evening will be worth less to him than 500 gold mohrs.

You will, perhaps, think I treat the subject very gayly. I do—in order to keep my mind clear of melancholy thoughts. The dear woman, that is now a saint in Heaven, approves the work I have accomplished ; and I am teaching myself to forget the grave, and look for her only in the bright regions of eternity.

On which accounts, it has been determined, no one of us shall visit the spot where her earthly remains are lodged. Mrs. Hartly affirms, it is flying in the face of Providence, to neglect the practice of resignation ; and Mrs. D—'s speaking silence seems to claim that respect from us, no language could have engaged for her. Sentimental sorrow, as Dr. Johnson calls it, is, I am now satisfied, the bane of happiness, in a wider degree than the worst evil under the sun, which that refinement is prompted to resist ; insomuch, that I hope you will find we have benefited by our voyage.

There are monsters, Arabella, in human shapes, and the Eastern world is (what I should have returned without conceiving it to be, but for the incident of this morning)

the scene of tragedies that dishonour mankind.—I have, within the passing hour, beheld one of these wretches conveyed to prison —and may condign punishment be his
portion !

He is, my dear, an officer in the army—who
having, in some of his country rides, discovered an old man's daughter to be lovely
beyond whatever this country has produced,
cruelly and basely resolved to rob him of her.
To her father's house he went, on this dia-
bolical design, and was received by its innocent and unsuspecting inhabitants with the
utmost kindness ;—in consequence of which
reception, he changed his plan of outrage—
and, instead of bearing her off, as he intended,
he settled it to violate the laws of hospitality
—of God and of man—and accomplish his
work of darkness under the paternal roof !

To win her, he found impossible—he therefore had recourse to violence ; and, when the
poor old man, terrified by his daughter's cries,
advanced to her assistance, he shot him dead
before his child's eyes ; and then proceeded
to fill up the measure of his iniquity. Yes !
Arabella ! the man whose profession it was
to protect, thus brutally and barbarously

destroyed !—May his name be branded with
infamy !—and his death be equally unpitied
and ignominious.—I now rejoice, more than
ever, that I am about to leave a country,
where fiend-like acts are, I fear, much oftener
perpetrated than detected ; for, the grave
complains not, and gold can unnerve the arm
of justice.—Lord C——will not, however,
stain his noble deeds, by suffering such a vil-
lain to escape ; and the facts I have related are
too well known, and too glaringly confirmed,
to be palliated, or atoned by less than the life
of him who could devise deeds of such turpi-
tude ; or, when even devised, could have the
savage nature to carry them into effect.—I
am all indignation, terror, compassion, and
agitation :—the young woman survives, however, to appal the guilty wretch by her melancholy testimony

———

We embark, Arabella, within the hour I
am now devoting to my pen ; and few evenings, I should suppose, produced more weddings, than took place three evenings ago at
Hartly House. Yes Arabella, I have been
three days a wife ; and so abundantly are my

family connections enlarged, that I have a mother I am proud to acknowledge, and sisters and brothers, in consequence of my change of condition ; for the sister of Mrs. Hartly is now Mrs. D——'s daughter, and inclination will convert an alliance into the ties of relationship, beyond legal claims :—and, Arabella, I bring over with me the man I have chosen for your husband, the celebrated Beville of our Calcutta theatre.—Be propitious, ye gales ; let not so much happiness be the prey of disaster !—But remember, Arabella, for your consolation, should we all be buried in the deep, that Providence has a right to dispose of us at will ; and that, however unable mortals are to penetrate Heaven's design, every seeming misfortune is a disguised blessing, to those who possess rectitude of heart and uprightness of conduct : such are kindly sheltered, by what is called a violent death, from the approaching, though unseen miseries of existence.

A thousand times farewell !

S. D.

LETTER XXXIX.

Portsmouth.

WE are all landed safe at this place, after a tedious, though not hazardous voyage. The addition of your company is ardently wished by every individual of the party to which I belong. Meet us then at Guildford, and augment the happiness of your own.

SOPHIA DOYLY.

AFTERWORD

Calcutta is a city inviting criticism, built on a disas-
trous site and now overcrowded beyond imagination.
Travellers hurry through censoriously and may be
forgiven for missing any sign that the original late
eighteenth-century Calcutta, wholly a creation of the
British, was a pleasant place of spacious houses, wide
streets and great gardens running down to the river,
and an equally uncrowded 'black town'. The battered
remains of these 'Hartly Houses' sometimes survive a
dirty accretion of more recent buildings, but it is now
almost impossible for a casual visitor to visualise what
the town looked like in 1786.

However, if you lived there the picture was different.
In retrospect it seems that in the thirteen years I spent
there, ending in 1953, the eighteenth century came
nearer to the twentieth, and the long heyday of the
Imperial Raj was the period which faded fastest. There
were three reasons for this. Politically the clocks went
back: those of the British community who went on
living and working in Calcutta were mainly merchants;

they were what the Company had set out to be, without the weight of governing India. They welcomed the independence of India in 1947. It became possible to concentrate on business, law or medicine, not to attempt, however unconsciously, to act a ruling role. It also became possible to take a deeper interest in Indian culture, which before independence was called 'getting a bit *deshi*' or 'going native', and to have friendships with Indians that had been barred by political considerations before independence.

Secondly, if you were prepared to look, particularly in dingy back streets, there were the artefacts of the eighteenth century everywhere. A poor country does not throw things away, they simply decline in the social scale. You could occasionally find decanters engraved with long forgotten regimental crests or blown-glass claret bottles, ranged between empty beer or ketchup bottles, in the lamp-lit alleys of the second-hand markets. (Stoppers were on the stall of another specialist.) You could find in other alleys books and prints, cut glass and furniture, ranging from the standard military chests made (as Sophia noted) by Chinamen, to elegant sofa tables and the heavy black-wood *almirahs* that the Portuguese made, carved with the *Roi Soleil* sunbursts that the French favoured.

And thirdly, perhaps even more pervasively, was the Calcutta social scene, as still played with deadly seriousness by the British and their associates in the Cold Weather. This formal and essentially frivolous round owed its origins to customs established before Sophia's day: mercantile precedence (or pecking-order), the balls, the races, the flirtations and the jealous inspection of those 'just out from Home' were as enduring a memorial to the eighteenth century as the mouldering palaces and tombstones of Park Street. Social Calcutta was always an unreal country:

> In various talk the instructive hours they passed
> Who gave the ball, or paid the visit last ...
> A third interprets motions, looks and eyes;
> At every word a reputation dies.
> Snuff or the fan supply each pause of chat
> With singing, laughing, ogling and all that ...

Sophia Goldborne has not only written the earliest fiction about this elegantly artificial scene, she also indicates the best way out of it by her tentative exploration of the real India.

Monica Clough, August 1989

NOTES

3. **packet ... from St Helena:** the account of the voyage out is given on p. 228, for no discernible reason, unless to underline the uncertainty of mails.

7. **Sawger:** *Saugor Island*, properly *Ganga Sagara* – Ocean Ganges, a landfall formerly a place of pilgrimage at the mouth of the Hoogly, suffering devastating cyclones, and with a large population of tiger and crocodile.
Alligators, referred to several times, is now a name only applied to American and African species.

8. **Bugeros:** a form of Ganges river-barge with shaded cabin accommodation aft. It was a compromise between Thames state barges and Bengali vessels, and usually rowed or tracked by a rope from the shore; occasionally a square sail was set. Not sea-worthy, very popular for parties of pleasure, and for longer journeys up-country, in roadless Bengal.

10. **Oroonoko:** a tragedy by Southern (1696), not particularly appropriate to Sophia's situation, turning on the fate of a fatherless beauty.
Loll Shrub: *Lal sharab*, or red wine, 'Englishman's hindi'.

11. **Kittesan:** or **Kittysol,** or **Kittysaw** (p. 70) spelt variously. A parasol of bamboo, paper or fabric universally in use; from Portuguese *quita-sol*, escape-the-sun.
Diamond Point: the author's geography is wildly inaccurate always. She is confusing Diamond

Harbour with Hoogly Point which was nearer Calcutta and a traditional meeting point. The distances she gives for *Culpee* and *Cudgerre* on p. 8 are also misleading.

Palanquin: sedan chairs adapted for four bearers can be seen in Daniells' prints of Calcutta in 1786, but the more popular form was a box with shaded sides, like a medieval litter, in which a journey of hundreds of miles was undertaken in the interior of India.

Har carrier: *Hakara* is a messenger, Sophia should have called the torch-bearers *masalchies*. In contemporary London they were called link-boys.

Tok, Tok: not a cry but a sound made by a small pair of clappers, still in use by rickshaw pullers.

'Auri veni (motalis)': a tag much quoted in the East: 'Come fleeting breeze'. One assumes Sophia had not read Ovid's *Ars Amatoris* where it first occurs.

12. **Hartly House**: the description is of a standard, almost modest, Calcutta mansion. Philip Francis in 1776 rented one of roughly twice these dimensions for £100 a month, needing 100 servants to maintain.

13. **The furniture was all Chinese**: there was much trade between Canton and Calcutta at this time, and furniture and china were freely imported. English furniture was also much imported, originally as cabin-furnishings. There were then few local cabinet-makers, in a land devoted to the use of bamboo.

    Musketto: mosquitoes are a lasting irritation in Bengal particularly to new arrivals: interesting that the author compares the annoyance with that of the bed-bugs of London.

14. Sophia must have arrived at the end of September 1784. The information she quotes is inaccurate: the 'Cold Weather' lasts from the end of September to the end of February, followed by the Hot Weather, which gets progressively hotter and more humid until the dramatic break of the rains about the first week of June.

16. **Hooka**: the description given is accurate. Quantities of eighteenth-century hooka-bases in silver, porcelain or bidri-metal, and in masculine and feminine sizes, were still to be found in second-hand bazaars up to the 1950s. Some were made in France, and some adorned with patriotic British roses and thistles. The custom of smoking them was rejected by refined Englishwomen in early Victorian times, though men kept it up for another couple of generations. A hooka requires its own servant, its *Hooka Burdar* to prepare and clean the equipment, and to keep the flame alight by fanning. The tobacco was also bought and prepared by the Burdar. The flame was given by a smouldering *goli* (ball) of rice-straw and resins. *Golis* stood on the tables of the Bengal Club until the 1950s, in silver *goli-dans* like corinthian columns, to provide lights for cigars. A hooka is said to be the healthiest way to smoke tobacco, as all the smoke is drawn through water, which congeals the tar, in the hooka-base.

17. **Country born**: Sophia's attitude to race is enigmatic. Here she approves a girl for her 'complexion near the European standard', but at least the girl was accepted as a member of the Hartly household.

18–19. **Hartly Mansion**: to get a view of the Esplanade, Hartly House is situated at the north end of Chowringee. *Chinam* (chunnam) was expensively made from sea-shells imported into Calcutta, and finely ground. Later, stucco lime-wash was substituted for use on walls, and annually renewed after the rains. T & W Daniell's prints of Calcutta in 1786 show that many newly-built mansions became dilapidated under the impact of sun and rain, then as now.

20. **Verandah**: the author appears to confuse *verandah* with shutter, the universal fixed Venetian blind, or persiane, made of wood and later called a *jhil-mhil* in India, though this word has not been traced before

1832. Perhaps *verandah* was in her day applied to the
shutters as well as to the gallery or portico which
they shaded, and which is still known as a verandah.
Glass for windows was scarce, expensive and unnecessary; gauze or bamboo matting was sometimes
used. The *Khus-Khus tatty* or screen of dampened
fragrant grasses was introduced to Calcutta in 1789,
and immediately became popular. The overhead
punkah was also introduced to Calcutta after Sophia's
day; the poor girl must have suffered from the unmit-
igated heat a good deal.

21. **The poet** is of course James Thomson. His 'Summer'
was first printed in 1727 and remained a favourite in
Georgian England.

24. **New church**: St John's (Cathedral, as it became) was
opened in 1787.

25. **Neatness ... virtue of cleanliness**: one of the last
governors of Bengal, the Australian Casey, remarked
that he had never seen such remarkable personal
cleanliness and corporate filth, as in Calcutta. The
corporate filth was largely the product of administrative inertia and industrialisation. The sanitation of
Calcutta, with no outfall and where drains still over-
flow backwards in high Spring tides, can never have
been adequate, but Georgian London was not a city
for the squeamish either.

26. **Moors and Gentoos**: *Moors* was the general term for
all moslems, *Gentoos* (from the Portuguese for
gentiles, heathens) for hindus.
Chapter and verse: A L Basham comments on this
passage that Sophia gives the historical priority of
Asia over Europe, and notes she closely links that
history with the Book of Genesis. He continues to
criticise, rightly, the inaccuracies about Indian
history: 'The latter statement shows that the author
was writing entirely from memory since a reference
to any one of several books on India current at the

time would have given accurate dates.' Sophia might indeed have referred to the three volumes of Orme's *History of Military Transactions*, J Z Holwell's *Historical Events relative to the Province of Bengal and Empire of Industan* or even more profitably to the Abbé Raynal's *Histoire philosophical et political des Européens dans les deux Indes*, of which the English translation appeared in London in 1772. Rennell's *Map of Bengal* was printed in 1781. It is obvious she had none of these at hand at the time of writing.

29. **Khouli Khan**: better known as Nadir Shah.

34. **A repast**: the mid-morning meal only became known as *Tiffen* long after this; the term evolved from early nineteenth-century English slang.

38–9. **The Household retinue**: this account is one of the most curious in a novel which promises to take you into a European household in Bengal. It is a front-of-house account, only of those whom a visitor would meet, and confirms suspicions that the book was written by a transient who had never kept house there. The actual list would have been much longer. *Seda-Bearer* is the *Sirdah* or head bearer, gentoo in her day perhaps, but moors (moslems) had less repugnance for European eating and bodily customs and so became more generally employed in the households of Bengal. The confusion between *harcarrie* and *mussalchie* noted above is repeated. But what about the kitchen, Miss Sophia? Cooks in Bengal received great honour from the rest of the staff (though they were in general Christian), and were customarily called *Caleefa* by the other servants, a corruption of *Khālif*. This worthy was supported by a team, usually of poor relations, of cooks' mates, carriers of the heavy baskets of produce home from the daily bazaar, and scullions. And did none of the Hartly women have an *Ayah* or ladies' maid, nor a *metherani* to sweep the floors, keep the bathroom clean and

remove ordure? And what about the *Durzi* or tailor
who sewed the multitude of muslin garments, and
who was sometimes rumoured to take advantage of
the close contact needed to measure their patrons
'round the neck' as a delicate account of 1813 put it?

Another omission is the *Dhobi* or washerman, and
the tribe of *bhistis* or water carriers who in Calcutta
went daily to the Lal Diggi, or great tank, to fill skins
with the heavily polluted water found there. And the
Head Groom she mentions, in his European way,
would have had a duplicate team of Indian *syces* or
grooms, together with humbler grass-cutters and
forage-gatherers actually to do the work, under his
supervision. An admirable list with aquatint illustra-
tions can be found in Charles D'Oyly, *The European In
India* (1813) and another, for Calcutta in the 1820s, is
given by Lady Fanny Park in *Wanderings of a Pilgrim
in Search of the Picturesque* (2 vols, 1850) and in
almost every other book of similar descriptive vein.

41. The exchange of **used teacups** in polite English
society is a formidable idea. Women playing cards for
high stakes was another and more welcome casualty
of Victorian memsahibs' morality; the custom however
returned in Edwardian days with the introduction of
contract bridge. For men's gambling and card-playing
the *Memoirs* of William Hickey provides ample
evidence. Philip Francis once claimed to have made
£20,000 from whist in a night in 1776.

44. **Notch-girls**, *Notchee, Nauch*: anglicised names for
dancing-girls from Hindi Nāch. In the eighteenth
and nineteenth centuries, the great classic hindu
form of *Bharat natyam* was in severe eclipse; a
debased form of *Khatak* or court dancing was popular
as an entertainment mainly given by wealthy Indians
for the titillation of Westerners.

Company's Gardens: name later given to the famous
Botanic Gardens at Sibpur, founded by Colonel Kyd

in 1786. Sophia could not have crossed the wide Hoogly River, even by moonlight, to reach non-existent gardens, and a more accessible Company Garden existed near the Fort.

46. James Thomson's *Seasons*: 'Summer', line, 663–89, is a good summary of some of the plants in a well-kept *phal-bagan* (orchard) in Bengal – with the exception of cocoa, which could not be encouraged to grow.

48. **For me the mine** ... : Pope's *Essay on Man*.

50. **Sacre rupees**: *Sicca* Rupees (arabic: coined money) were fractionally heavier silver than the many other varieties of rupees then current. Standardisation was not achieved until 1836, with 'the Company Rupee'.

Beisars: the *bazaar* is the quarter in which specialist Indian tradesmen congregate. Sophia gives a few examples, *Bada Besar* is obscure, she may mean either the big bazaar, or the *Bhāt bazaar* (*Bhāt* is Bengali for rice, and by extension, all foodstuffs). *Muche* is Bengali for fish, *māchchi*; a *dewdwallar* is the milkman, *dhood walla*; *suedwaller besar* would have been a collection of outcastes of both major faiths, who dealt in forbidden pork. *Chine* bazaar might be for *Chhini*, sugar, or China, as the *Old China Bazaar* was a well-known shopping area behind the Armenian Church. *Dahi*, or curds, is a staple of the Bengali diet.

51. **Europe shops**: the custom of the day was to use nouns for adjectives of place, e.g. 'India muslin'. The 'mark-up' on imported goods was always notorious.

Five Streets: these still form the hub of Calcutta and may be studied as they appear in Sophia's account in the prints of Calcutta by T & W Daniell in 1786 to 1789. The streets were then called Esplanade running up from the river past Government House and the Council House, and a grid leading off it, then named Durrumtollah, Cossitola, Court House and Council House streets, the latter leading to Tank Square, with

Writers' Buildings, and Post Office Street and ruins of the Old Fort.

57. **Gentoo phrases**: another enigma of this book is what amount, if any, did Sophia learn of Hindi, Bengali or Court Persian during her stay? Hardly any from internal evidence. Her first conversations with 'my Bramin' were through an interpreter (p. 124); later he seems to speak English to her (p. 185).

58. **Calcutta Theatre**: Sophia makes many references to what was obviously a major social attraction. Performances were given by casts of male amateurs, though these were challenged by Miss Wrangham, a celebrated beauty, who married impeccably high-up Mr Bristow in the 1780s and proceeded to set up a private theatre and to act there. Miss Wrangham's nickname and exploits fill pages of the scurrilous *Bengal Gazette*. Sophia visited the theatre in Lyon's Range, which flourished between 1775 and 1808. A ballroom, frequently used for polite assemblies, was attached.

59. **The London Hotel**: *London Tavern* on the south side of the Tank Square, and a competing *Harmonic Tavern* were well frequented.

Calcutta Advertiser, Chronicle, etc.: Sophia is understandably confused. A number of transient papers followed Hicky's short-lived and far from 'moral' *Gazette*. This Hicky is not to be confused with the Calcutta contemporary William Hickey whose *Memoirs* 1745–1808 (4 vols) were not published until 1923. The latter was a barrister and, if as dissolute as the journalist, more successful, though by the time Sophia is in Calcutta Hickey had withdrawn from polite society, mourning his dead Charlotte (in the Park Street cemetery) and consoling himself with the bottle and a 'convenient' (a black dancer) in his *bibikhana*, 'women's quarters', but most of all with professional legal gossip about the affairs of the High

Court and Bar. Hicky the journalist eventually went too far and was thrown into jail, nominally for debt. Sophia's papers were the sedate *India Gazette* starting in November 1780 and containing official intimations and the *Oriental Advertiser*. The *Calcutta Chronicle* began publication in January 1786.

60. **Hospital**: see also pp. 74–5 and note. The Company Hospital (later known as the Presidency General Hospital) was opened on the south side of the Maidan in a garden house in 1768, to take the place of one handily close to St John's burial ground in the city centre, of which Hamilton wrote in 1717 'many go in to undertake the penance of Physic but few come out to give an account of its operation'.

   The Black Hole: Sophia follows the standard account of this humiliating episode by J Z Holwell, a survivor. His account is now considered exaggerated. *Mhir Jaffier* (Mir Jafar) in a throw-away phrase is described as 'a friend to the English'. The whole episode, culminating in the British victory at Plassey in 1757, was the Asian part of the global struggle with France in the Seven Years' War. British success ushered in a period of unprincipled extortion by Company servants and independent merchants in Bengal.

63. **Bungilo**: the English *bungalow* is a borrow-word from 'bangala', Bengali-style, applied to the kind of one-storey villa she describes. Garden houses were popular and considered more healthy than town houses.

67. **The Nabob**: Nawab Nazim Mobaruk-ud-Doula, son of Mir Jafir, Nawab of Murshidabad and nominal Viceroy to the Mogul Emperor. Administration of the Revenue had recently passed to the British. He had property in Chitpore, North Calcutta. At the time of his visit to Warren Hastings in 1786, which Sophia describes, the Nawab-Sahib was 28 years old. The British collected the revenues of Bengal and paid him a large allowance.

69. **Such charioteers** and the preceding lines on p. 69
    are from Young's *Love of Fame, the Universal Passion*.

70. **Lady Chambers**: almost a catty reference to a
    reigning 'Burra Bibi'. Miss Fanny Wilton married in
    1774, after a brief career as an artists' model (Reynolds
    painted her as Hebe). She was 15 at the time of her
    marriage to Sir William Chambers, who was 20 years
    older and to whom she was devoted. Thus she was
    placed about third in the jealously guarded Table of
    Precedence, as her husband was a High Court Judge.
    Ten years on, she probably barely acknowledged
    newcomers to Calcutta like the unmarried Sophia.
    She even found it difficult to acknowledge Maria
    Imhoff when she became Mrs Warren Hastings.
    East India captain: a key rank in the East India
    Company's service, rating a 17-gun salute on coming
    ashore and ranking with Members of Council. With
    the perquisites of ullage and dunnage, i.e. stowing of
    private cargo for free carriage, captains became very
    wealthy. It is to be doubted, however, that this was
    Mr Goldborne's profession. A sojourn of nearly two
    years ashore in Bengal points more to an independ-
    ent merchant.

72. **The New Fort** was begun in 1757 after Plassey,
    completed about 1781, in the grand style of Vauban
    already made quite obsolete by artillery. This is the
    reason for the immense field of fire kept clear on the
    perimeter, the Maidan.

73. **Batta-money**: a special allowance which became
    permanent and a source of frequent dispute up to the
    Mutiny; probably from *Bhāt*, rice or food.

74. **Hospital**: see note p. 60. A hospital for the 'Relief of
    the Native Inhabitants' was opened in 1793.

78. **Bugee-Bugee**: as usual Sophia's sense of direction has
    let her down. *Budge-Budge* is 15 miles down river,
    Chitpore four miles in the opposite direction, north of
    central Calcutta.

80. **Othello**: did the well-read girl not have a copy of Shakespeare's Works handy?

83. **Salam ... chit**: Sophia has got it right this time.

88. **Sekar**: *Sircar* from Persian meaning *Head of Affairs*, applied (1) as here, to a house-steward or accountant in charge of household and business finances; (2) a moslem administrative division of territory; (3) Hindi slang name for government, *The Sircar*. Charles D'Oyly in *The European in India* (1813) hopes that 'this formidable gang of public and private dependers may speedily become extinct' and goes on to condemn the hold 'about twenty years back' (that is, in Sophia's day) of these money dealers, who often, he claims, retired on their gains to become *Shroffs* or money-lenders, and who all manipulated the exchange rates of the many currencies to their own advantage. Mr Goldborne seems to have considered himself more lucky in his Sircar than this. See p. 243, letter XXXIII.

89. **Celibate**: celibacy is unusual amongst Bramins, and is not a religious obligation.

92. **Thomson's** *Seasons*, 'Summer', lines 784–90.

93. **Trees of Destruction**: not the site of the celebrated duel between Warren Hastings and Philip Francis in 1780, which was across the nullah in Alipore, but trees traditionally associated with duels still grown on the site she indicates.

97. **Golconda diamonds**: the famous mines were then nearly worked out. Tavernier gives a first-hand account of them 100 years before. Far from walking unscathed, Indian travellers of this date were at the mercy of *dacoits* (bands of thieves) and *Thugs* who murdered travellers as a religious obligation.

99. **A holy text**: a misquotation from Gray's *Elegy*.

100. **Burying grounds**: since the 1960s, the surviving South Park Street Burial Grounds have been restored from deep neglect, and are still remarkable for the

'obelisks, pagodas, etc' that she mentions and for the virtually total lack of any Christian iconography. Job Charnock, founder of Calcutta, used to sacrifice a cock annually here, on the grave of the Bramini wife he rescued from Sāti. The graves remain the most powerful memorials of the Age of Reason in Calcutta.

103. **Thomas Arne:** (1710–77), a prolific and popular composer. *Artaxerxes* (1762) was 'an English opera from the Italian of Metastasio'.

104. **The Governor's dress:** an abrupt introduction to Warren Hastings on the eve of his departure after 13 years as Governor of Bengal Presidency. He dressed and lived unostentatiously, 'a plain looking man in a brown coat'. A modern historian has written: 'Since Akbar no one of this stature has walked the Indian stage' (P Woodruffe, *The Men who Made India,* vol. I, p. 122).

    His lady: Maria Imhoff, née Chapusettin, wife of a German miniature painter trying his fortune in India. Both travelled out in the same ship as Hastings in 1772; later, after divorcing Imhoff, she and Hastings were married and Maria became First Lady. After this equivocal start she was (perforce) accepted, and played her part with panache. Surviving letters of both the Hastings show their deep attachment.

111. **The padre:** Sophia never misses an opportunity to make a cut at the Presidency Chaplain, who at this time was the Reverend 'Tally-Ho!' Johnston, a robust eighteenth-century cleric, who retired in the 1790s with a fortune.

    The head gardener – a botanist: Hartly House gardens were lucky. Possibly there may have been an educated half-caste or Portuguese employed over the team of *malis*, otherwise Sophia would have found language an insurmountable barrier to botany.

114. **Ices:** Fanny Parks gives an account and a lithograph of ice-making in the Cold Weather on the outskirts of Calcutta (vol. I, p. 76).

115. **London porter:** the recent discovery that beer would travel in bottles enormously enlarged the market for British commercial brewers, hence India Pale Ale, 'Porter' because it was portable. Stout was the first to be bottled, and hence became known as Porter.
116. **Summer:** Thomson again.
119. **Jerry Blackacre:** from Wycherley's *Plain Dealer*, a mother-dominated dim wit.
120. **Feathered tribes:** an improbable lot of birds for an aviary. The last bird to domesticate in Calcutta would be a *Bramini Kite* (Haliastur indus) a ruthless and very common bird, one of the scavengers of the country.
121. **Jerry Daw's soldiers:** the Adjutant stork (Leptoptilos dubius, Hindi *Hargili*) was an even more voracious scavenger which stalked about fearlessly, eating carrion in the streets.
122. **Lawyers:** the best description of the Calcutta Bar and of lawyers' gossip in the 1780s is to be found in the pages of William Hickey's *Memoirs*. Sophia's account is fair enough.
123. **Sekar:** see note, p. 88.
124. **Bramin:** the twice-born priestly caste. The *Gentoo university at Benares*. *Varansi* (Benares) was then as now renowned as a holy city for hindus. The 'university' cannot now be identified from the number of Bramin places of learning there. Lay Bramins often opened eating houses, as they cooked superlatively well, and no contamination could be suffered by anyone who ate Bramin food. The provision of plates of leaves and throw-away cups of earthenware saved the Bramin from contamination by his customers.
   Sittris: *Kshattriya*, originally warriors.
   Besia: *Vaisya*, merchant castes. Goldborne's *Sekar* must, unusually, have been a Bramin, to have had a twice-born nephew.
125. **Sudder:** *the Sudra* – the lowest rung of the caste system, the peasantry.

Atarris: *Hari* (Bengali for refuse collectors) – the outcast sweepers or Harrys of European households. Gandhi renamed them **Hari-Jan**, the people of God, in an effort to restore some status to these 'untouchables'.

128. **Brumma:** Brahma, the Supreme Being, impossible to reduce to a footnote.

Vidam: *The Veda,* the four sacred books of Bramin teaching. Their existence (but not their contents) was well-known in the eighteenth century. The stories of the Mahabarata, etc. were embedded in Indian consciousness and would have passed into the European mind through the Indians who brought up European children and sang them to sleep with stories of *Sita-Rama.* Even the passing military man would have noticed the forms of the different deities in wayside statues, but the underlying philosophies and the authentic early documents had to wait for the patient studies of Sir William Jones, Halhed, and other Orientalists encouraged by Warren Hastings to unravel and translate them. Indians as well as the West are indebted to their scholarship. The Royal Asiatic Society was founded in Calcutta in 1786.

Shahstah: A truly alarming mis-spelling, in a quasi-moslem form, of **Sastra**, sanskrit for a Rule: the hindu code book.

135. **Tigers:** Sophia's attitude to tiger-shikar (hunting) was unusual and commendable, influenced by hindu beliefs in non-violence and reincarnation.

137. **His Majesty's Coronation:** celebration of this anniversary was made annually in all overseas British possessions.

139. **Gentoo holidays:** the September and October *Puja* season of celebrations of Durga, the defeat of Ravana, and the invocations of the goddesses of learning and wealth. The hindus of Bengal make a practice of

immersing specially constructed idols of each deity in the Ganges at the close of the festival.

Guido Reni: Italian painter of soulful saints, over praised and much collected by Englishmen who had made the Grand Tour.

141. **Sacred rivers**: enormous as their catchment areas are, these rivers are not handy or indeed necessary for the ceremonial needs of the subcontinent.

Better to sit, etc.: this is said by A L Basham to be the first recorded instance of a proverb which was later much quoted, usually pejoratively.

142. **The Company**: Sophia's figures are tolerably accurate. She delicately indicates that 'portable eastern bribes' and other temptations added to the personal wealth of the Company servants.

146. **Mrs Hartly's closet**: a small room with walls pasted with prints in paper-printed frames was a fashionable foible in England. *Marchioness of Tavistock* was a recently-dead beauty, the *Royal victim* may be Caroline Matilda, sister of George III, married to and disowned by a King of Denmark and dead at 24. Sophia's description could almost equally well apply to Mary Queen of Scots; all that matters is the refined taste shown by Mrs Hartly.

148. **'A whole length'** is of *Mrs Elisabeth Montague* who wrote an *Essay on the Genius of Shakespeare.*

154. **Omar ... Hali**: Sophia makes a shot at distinguishing the largely *Sunni* moslems of Mogul India from the *Shia* (from 'sect' in Arabic) who count the orthodox descent of the Caliphate through *Ali*, and were mostly to be found then in Turkey and Persia.

158. **Watson's Works**: Colonel H Watson became Chief Engineer in Calcutta in 1765 and established docks at Kidderpore in 1780. Never as successful as the docks in Bombay which built East Indiamen and, later, battleships for Nelson, Watson built river boats, bugeros and pinnaces, and sadly went bankrupt,

bequeathing his name to the neighbouring *Watgunge*.

175. **Alligators ... disposal of the dead**: crocodiles, in point of fact. The scarcity of firewood made orthodox cremation always expensive until coal-gas was laid on to the burning ghats at Nimtalla. However, charred and partly consumed corpses are still launched into the Hoogly, and are disposed of by crocodile, vulture and jackal.

Those wives who commit Sāti. Abolished (with difficulty) in British India during Bentick's administration in 1820s.

177. **Barbarous exhibition**: *Chharak puja* when votaries suspend their bodies by a hook through (usually) the back muscles, and are hoisted to revolve round an overhead wheel. Still performed in remote corners of Bangladesh by a hindu minority.

187. **Mrs H**: Mrs Hastings, accompanied by Mrs Motte as companion, actually set sail in January 1784, and Warren Hastings left over a year later, February 1785. Mrs H's fare on the *Atlas* Indiaman was the huge sum of Rs 40,000 sicca (£7,000) plus Rs 1,000 for Mrs Motte.

188. **To Sawger**: an exaggeration, it was not possible to sail a river bugero into the tidal currents below Diamond Harbour. Hastings records he said his farewells from a pinnace at Culpee, further up-river.

193. **Rajapoots**: Rajput 'the sons of kings'. Colonel Todd's *Annals of Rajastan* were published in 1829, recording their history and martial lifestyle.

194. **Omrah – Mirza – jaghire**: Sophia is on the right lines.

195: **Love in the Village**: a favourite comic opera by Bickerstaffe (1763), already performed during Sophia's visit.

200. **Boarding school**: at least five boarding schools for young ladies are recorded before 1800 in Calcutta. The social implications of giving a daughter a merely

'country' education had to be weighed against the great cost of passages to England. See *Mrs Savage*, pp. 245–6.

202. **The present Governor:** Sir John Macpherson, of the Company's Civil Service governed for the 20 months before Hastings' successor, Lord Cornwallis, arrived in 1786.
Young Meadows etc: the play was *Love in a Village*.

217. **Her physician:** no likely name can now be found for this practitioner.

220. **The Tide of the Ganges:** wrong again. Naturally it never flowed backwards, but during the three midsummer months of the Rains the flood water made it impassable to sailing ships; the Hoogly is also subject to predictable and very large bore-tides, when a wave of up to 8 foot high sweeps up the river, causing much damage.

222. **Public prison:** the civil prison was in Lall Bazaar, opened in 1782. There was a country jail near Park Street where the journalist Hicky endured confinement with his wife and some of his 12 children. (British jails were then much the same.)

226. **The Gentoo university:** the moslem rulers of Bengal encouraged a Vidalaya or hindu university at Nadia.

229. **St Johanne:** is actually on the other side of Africa, nearer Madagascar than the Madeiras. The rest of the account is tolerable, including the landing at *Madras*, p. 231. An upset surf-boat was far too common a hazard to risk the loss of skilled boatmen through capital punishment.

230. **Balagant:** more correctly *Balaghat*, a name then given to the great spine of mountains dividing *Coromandel* (Madras side) now Tamil Nadu, from the western coastal strip, now Karnata and Kerala (Travancore.)

241. **Belate Be Bee:** the foreign (English) lady. *Wilayat*: Arabic/Persian for a Kingdom, i.e. Britain; *Bibi*, the

same language, an honorific for a lady. Both words became further debased, *Belate* became *Blighty*, for white soldiers, and *Bibi* became a polite way of describing an Indian mistress, and therefore was unsuitable for 'pukka' wives who became *Memsahibs*, a hybrid 'Englished' title.

Chookalo Calaloo is garbled beyond recognition.

243. **Sekar:** see note on p. 88.

264. **Lord Cornwallis:** arrived September 1786. The Hartly House party were in one of many attendant bugeros. The State bugero was magnificent and 'Elephant-headed'.

269. **Letter XXXVII:** the Nawab's visit to Lord Cornwallis is juxtaposed with the episode in the next letter of the rape of an Indian girl by an English officer. The contrast is only implied. Sophia has lost her heart to an India she considers to be full of gentle beings, and is out of patience with many of her compatriots.